Praise for
Mike Hernacki's

THE ULTIMATE SECRET
TO GETTING ABSOLUTELY
EVERYTHING YOU WANT:

"FILLED WITH WISDOM
AND COMMON SENSE . . .
A SECRET THAT REALLY WORKS."
—NORMAN VINCENT PEALE

"DO WHATEVER IT TAKES
TO READ THIS BOOK."
—CLARENCE G. CATALLO,
Senior Vice-President,
Paine Webber, Inc.

"ABSOLUTELY WONDERFUL!
IT IS REALLY 'THE SECRET'
AND THE ABSOLUTE TRUTH."
—BETTY DODDS, Publicist,
Literary Promotions Network

"IT HAS HELPED ME MORE
THAN ANYTHING ELSE
I HAVE *EVER* READ."
—D. FAAST

Berkley Books by Mike Hernacki

THE FORGOTTEN SECRET TO PHENOMENAL SUCCESS

THE SECRET TO CONQUERING FEAR

THE ULTIMATE SECRET TO GETTING
ABSOLUTELY EVERYTHING YOU WANT

THE SECRET TO PERMANENT PROSPERITY

THE
SECRET
TO
PERMANENT
PROSPERITY

MIKE
HERNACKI

BERKLEY BOOKS, NEW YORK

THE SECRET TO PERMANENT PROSPERITY

A Berkley Book / published by arrangement with
the author

PRINTING HISTORY
Berkley edition / November 1994

ISBN: 0-425-14463-1

BERKLEY®
Berkley Books are published by The Berkley Publishing Group,
200 Madison Avenue, New York, New York 10016.
BERKLEY and the "B" design
are trademarks belonging to Berkley Publishing Corporation.

PRINTED IN THE UNITED STATES OF AMERICA

10 9 8 7 6 5 4 3 2 1

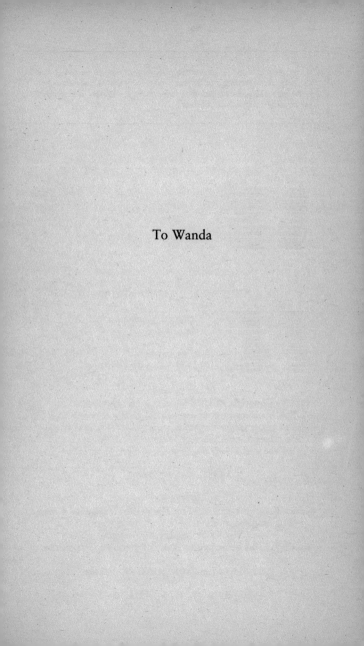

To Wanda

ACKNOWLEDGMENTS

A book is the tip of an iceberg. What you see is a few thousand words credited to a single author. What you don't see is the huge amount of effort on the part of many people, over several years. Even a small book like this is a big project, and it's impossible to acknowledge everyone who helped make it happen.

Still, I'd be remiss if I didn't thank at least a few marvelous people: Sandy Dijkstra, the world's greatest literary agent; Hillary Cige, the world's greatest editor; Keri Sims, the world's greatest assistant. Also Gerrit Borg, Bobbi DePorter, Vicki Gibbs, Roger Lane, Brian Lepis, Kathy Saideman, Steve Shapiro and Ed Watkins.

I wish I could show this book to my late mother, Phyllis Hernacki, and thank her in person for teaching me the most important, most profound principles of prosperity in a little family grocery store. The people who run the world's biggest corporations could have taken a few lessons from her. Thanks, Ma; you were right.

CONTENTS

CHAPTER 1 The Promise of Prosperity 1

CHAPTER 2 Money Has Nothing to Do With It 13

CHAPTER 3 Born to Be Prosperous 23

CHAPTER 4 Do You Really Want Prosperity? 31

CHAPTER 5 A Simple Secret 41

CHAPTER 6 The Road to Prosperity Is Paved With Value 55

CHAPTER 7 Developing Your Prosperity Consciousness 65

CHAPTER 8 Changing One Thing Changes Everything 73

CHAPTER 9 You Have to Give Before You Get 85

CHAPTER 10 What If Your Prosperity Goes Away? 97

CHAPTER 11 What If You Hate Your Prosperity? 105

CHAPTER 12 Believe In the System—It Always Works 111

THE
SECRET
TO
PERMANENT
PROSPERITY

The Promise of Prosperity

"Only learn to seize good fortune, for good fortune's always here."

—GOETHE

Imagine what your life would be like if you were truly prosperous. Imagine you had more than enough of everything you need, and the means to get everything you want—health, happiness, wealth, success. Imagine all of these flowing to you in a steady stream—sometimes faster, sometimes slower, but never stopping as long as you live. How would you feel if your life was like that?

If you can imagine such a scenario, if you can conjure up such a feeling—however vague it may be—then you have what it takes to create prosperity in your life. Because the truth is, prosperity is available to anyone who wants it.

No matter what your age, or where you live, or how much education you have, you can become prosperous, starting right now. Your prosperity doesn't depend on economic conditions; you can become prosperous in good times and bad. It doesn't matter how much money you have or how many people you know or how hard you work. To become prosperous, you don't need investment capital or influential contacts. To become prosperous, you don't have to work hard. In fact, you may not have to work at all. Many people have become prosperous without doing a minute of what is commonly known as work.

Does any of this surprise you? Well, it's just the beginning. Before you finish reading this book, you may be even more surprised to learn that:

- Prosperity isn't what you think it is.
- Prosperity can't be found where you've been looking.
- Prosperity isn't created in the way you believe it is.

Before you finish reading this book, you may have to throw away all your old notions about prosperity. But that's okay, because if you're not already prosperous, then your old notions haven't done you much good. On the other hand, if you *are* already prosperous, this book will help you make your prosperity *permanent*.

What if you're not prosperous, and you just can't imagine being that way? What if poverty, scarcity and struggle are so much a part of your life you can't picture living without them? Read this book anyway. By the time you're done, that mind-set will probably change. And for your sake, I hope it does, because if you can't imagine what it's like to be prosperous, you'll spend the rest of your life taking orders from someone who can.

HOW DO YOU MEASURE PROSPERITY?

For most people, the word "prosperity" has almost the same meaning as the word "money." In fact, a desire for more money may be what sparked your interest in a book about prosperity. If so, fine. It's a good enough place to start.

If "prosperity" means "money," then as Americans, we should be able to measure prosperity merely by counting our dollars. And we have a lot of them to count: In terms of dollars, the period since the end of World War II has been the most prosperous time in American history.

Let's start with the Gross National Product (GNP), which is the money value of all the products and services produced in a country in one year. In 1945, the United States' GNP was $197.3 billion. In 1990 (the most recent year for which I could get well-established numbers), it was $5.524 *trillion*. That's over *twenty-eight times* the 1945 figure. But wait; we have to adjust for inflation. There are a number of different ways to calculate the effect of inflation, so to be on the safe side, I'm using conservative assumptions. I'm calculating in a way that will produce a low result, to understate, rather than overstate, our prosperity.

When we factor in the effects of inflation, the dollar Americans carried in their pockets in 1945 was worth about eleven cents in 1990. Put another way, the lunch that cost you nine dollars in 1990 would have set you back just one dollar in 1945. That means the 1990 GNP is equal to about 607 billion of those 1945 dollars. Thus, the economy multiplied a little more than three times (607 billion, the inflation-adjusted 1990 GNP, is a little more than three times 197 billion, the 1945 GNP).

In 1945, the U.S. population was about 133 million. In 1990, it was a little less than twice that— about 250 million. So during the forty-five years after World War II, the economy *tripled* while the population *doubled*. The 1990 economy was creating substantially more wealth per person than the 1945 economy did—about a dollar and a half for every dollar. Statistically at least, it was creating about 50 percent more "prosperity."

But those statistics apply to the nation as a whole. They don't tell us how the individual was doing. To find out, we should compare something everyone can relate to, like annual personal income. In 1945, the per capita income in the U.S. was $1,117. In 1990, it was $14,420 (adjusted for inflation, $1,586). Translation: Folks in 1990 made about 40 percent more money than folks in 1945.

To illustrate this with an everyday example, let's say that in 1945 a cabdriver earned one dollar for driving a passenger from First Avenue to Tenth Avenue. A cabdriver in 1990 would have earned about $1.40 (in 1945 dollars) for doing exactly the same thing. The effort involved in getting a passenger from First to Tenth would be nearly identical, but he would have had 40 percent more to show for it than his 1945 counterpart.

This increased "prosperity" has shown up in the number of possessions Americans acquire. Per capita, today we own far more of everything than our parents and grandparents did: cars, trucks, motorcycles, recreational vehicles, boats—and those are just the big items. Consider some numbers:

- In 1945, there was one telephone for every five people in the United States; today there are more telephones than people—far more.
- In 1945, there were virtually no television sets in the United States. By 1970, there were 82.6 million. That's an average of 1.4 sets per household. From 1970 to 1990, the number of American households grew by some 51 percent. During that period, the number of television sets grew by 135 percent, to 193.2 million—or an average of 2.1 sets per household.
- In 1980, 1.1 percent of all the households that had a TV also had a videocassette recorder. By 1990, that figure was nearly 72 percent. And today . . . well, how many people do you know who don't have at least one VCR?

IS THE PROMISE OF PROSPERITY BEING KEPT?

The promise of prosperity has thus been offered to more people for longer than ever before in history. In the United States, we're so accustomed to things getting better and better, we've come to expect it. Yet as I write this, we're being told we can't expect permanent prosperity anymore.

Since the massive economic boom of the 1980's, a number of financial experts have been telling us our prosperity has topped out and is headed downward. Few of us will be as well-off as our parents, they say. In support of this argument, they point to the declining percentage of young people who can afford homes. They cite the number of women who must go to work just to make ends meet. They quote the slowing rates of economic growth, and paint pictures of an American Dream that's fading before our eyes.

Well, I disagree. On average, our fathers worked many more hours each week than we do. They owned far fewer cars, and they waited until they were much older before buying them. No matter what your age, chances are your father couldn't afford labor-saving appliances and home entertainment devices as early in life as you did.

Nor were our mothers' lives as easy as the lives of today's women. Yes, fewer married women worked outside the home a generation ago. But were these women sitting around drinking coffee with the neighbors all day? No, they were sewing clothes, knitting sweaters, darning socks, canning fruit, washing, ironing, baking bread from scratch, cooking nearly every family meal at home—and walking or taking the bus nearly everywhere they went, in every kind of weather.

Do today's married women work because one income isn't enough to live on? Or do more of them work because one income isn't enough to support the lifestyle we've gotten used to? While TVs and VCRs have multiplied like electronic rabbits, sewing machines have virtually disappeared from the American home. Your mother, like mine, may have owned a sewing machine. Your grandmother almost certainly did. Do you?

One out of two meals is now eaten in restaurants.

A generation ago, that ratio was far, far smaller. How many people do you know who carry their lunch to work every day? When our fathers were our age, how many people did *not* carry their lunch?

Compare your life with your father's—as to possessions, employee benefits, leisure time, and any other measures of prosperity you can think of. Then ask yourself if you'd change places with his generation.

True, we have high unemployment, but if you look through the newspapers of twenty and thirty years ago, as I have, you'll find there was unemployment then, too. And with the safety nets built into our system, even unemployment isn't as scary today as it was in our fathers' day.

Some people *were* better off twenty years ago than we are now. But on the average life has never been better, and as a nation we've never been more prosperous—at least materially—than at this moment.

People who would have us believe that the American Dream is disappearing are people who have forgotten *how* to dream. They are people who ignore the wealth of opportunity all around us; people who are looking for prosperity in all the wrong places.

But even if I'm right—even if the average person is better off today—does that mean *everyone* is better off? Because the average household has an automobile, several phones, two TVs and a VCR, does that make us all prosperous? Afraid not. Averages are mathematical terms. In *people* terms, while prosperity has proliferated, poverty has stubbornly persisted.

According to the U.S. Census Bureau, there were more Americans—35.7 million—living in pover

1991 than in any year since 1964, when President Lyndon Johnson launched his "War on Poverty." While that figure is disturbing, it does have a brighter side. The 35.7 million make up just 13.5 percent of the total population, whereas in 1964 the poor were 19 percent of the total and in 1959, they amounted to 22.4 percent.

While being poor has never been easy, there's more help available to the needy today than ever before. In 1989, the federal government doled out over three times as much public aid (adjusted for inflation) as it did in 1944. State and local governments spent over *twenty times* as much (also adjusted for inflation) as they did forty-five years earlier.

The number of blacks living in poverty has stayed about the same since 1959 (though the percentage has dropped from 55.1 to 31.9). The number of poor Hispanics has increased—both in actual numbers, and as a percentage of the population.

You could explain this by pointing out that blacks and Hispanics are discriminated against. Yet a fairly large number of whites (who presumably are not subject to such discrimination) have stayed below the poverty level: 22.3 million in 1990, versus 28.5 million in 1959.

How can so many people stay poor while so many others are becoming "prosperous?" Is there a basic difference between people who become prosperous and people who don't—a difference not related to economic opportunity or skin color? Could it be that prosperity and money are not synonymous after all? Before we answer, let's look at this issue from another angle.

WHEN "POOR" PEOPLE COME INTO MONEY

Since I write books about success and achievement, I'm keenly interested in all the money-making systems that are marketed today. I've found hundreds of get-rich books in libraries and bookstores. I've reviewed dozens of audiotapes and videotapes. I've watched endless late-night television "infomercials" telling people how to make fortunes in real estate and mail order. In every case, the author or promoter gives advice on how to accumulate wealth, assuming that once you, the customer, become rich, you'll happily stay that way forever.

But is this a correct assumption, I wondered? Does a sudden attainment of great wealth bring prosperity with it?

In doing research for this book, I found that this assumption is not only incorrect, it's downright dangerous. Throughout history, inheritors of great wealth have been notorious for spending and losing the fortunes they did nothing to acquire. Family lawyers created the "spendthrift trust" to protect these people from themselves. Stories of idle heirs wasting away their lives have been part of our literature for centuries.

In recent years, the most dramatic examples of people who have gotten rich quick are lottery winners. Never in history have so many "poor" people come into so much money in so little time.

I use the word "poor" to describe these people because English doesn't have a word that means the opposite of prosperous. Actually, most lottery winners are not poverty-stricken; they're working folks who on average tend to be at the lower end of the income spectrum.

I had heard that an alarming percentage of lottery winners actually went broke within a few years after hitting it big. In trying to verify this, I contacted a number of state lottery offices, and found that although they keep track of winners' addresses, lottery officials don't routinely follow up and see how their instant millionaires are doing financially. So reliable numbers are hard to come by.

But I did find in *The Psychonomy Journal* excerpts from a report titled, "Winning the Lottery is the Worst Thing That Can Ever Happen to You." The report provides evidence that a sudden overdose of money can produce a diminished sense of reality. In large enough infusions, instant wealth can cause severe mental impairment, and even death. Scientists at the Center for Psychiatric and Economic Fusion in Palo Alto, California, have dubbed this phenomenon "Post Cash Syndrome," or PCS.

Individual instances of PCS are frightening. One $2 million winner in Georgia went from being a mild-mannered computer technician to a wild-spending, obnoxious drunk who eventually killed himself by jumping from the top of his house into his empty, whale-shaped swimming pool.

While this is an extreme example, there are many more reports of people who spent and borrowed so heavily, they had to sign over the rights to all their future lottery checks just to get relief from constant badgering by their creditors. For numerous lottery winners, the changes brought about by their sudden wealth led to physical illnesses, divorces and estrangement from their families. Others, who realized they had no stomach for managing large amounts of money, simply gave it away rather than suffer the anxiety of dealing with it. Instead of bringing them prosperity, money brought them only misery.

A newspaper in California conducted an informal poll of financial planners who give advice to lottery winners and heirs of large estates. In describing these people's reactions to their sudden wealth, the financial planners most often mentioned:

- fear of handling the money improperly;
- guilt at not having earned it;
- distrust and paranoia as friends and relatives besiege them with advice and requests.

Perhaps most disturbing of all, some of the "lucky" ones allow the wealth to sap their personal drive. They lose their motivation, and just drift through life.

People in these circumstances can hardly be called prosperous. Yet by the standard measure—dollars and cents—all the statisticians would put them in that category. Wouldn't you?

A QUEST, AND A DISCOVERY

So far, looking at prosperity has yielded us more questions than answers:

- Why have some people stayed poor even though as a country we've enjoyed more than fifty years of steadily increasing economic prosperity?

- Is there a basic difference between people who become prosperous and people who don't—an *internal* difference, not related to conditions outside themselves?
- Are there ways to measure prosperity other than by counting money and possessions?
- Can prosperity do you more harm than good?
- Why does prosperity elude some people even *after* they come into a substantial amount of money?

I've studied these questions for years. I've interviewed hundreds of people, read more books and articles than I can count and delved deeply into my own attitudes about prosperity. In the course of this searching, I've discovered a Secret—a simple, beautiful Secret that contains the answers to all these questions, and more.

I call it the Secret to Permanent Prosperity because once you know it, you'll have all you need to become prosperous. Once you've learned to use it, you'll be able to find it and hold on to your prosperity for the rest of your life. And to start the whole process, all you have to do is read this one little book.

Money Has Nothing to Do With It

> *"The man who has no money is poor, but the one who has nothing but money is poorer."*
> —ORISON SWETT MARDEN

If you're like most people, when someone mentions the word "prosperity," you think of money, financial wealth or material possessions. That's understandable. Even the dictionary casts its definition in those terms. My big Random House unabridged version says prosperity is a "successful, flourishing, or thriving condition, *esp. in financial respects*" (emphasis mine). I suspect people think of prosperity in terms of money for the simple reason that money is measurable. You can count it. There's no faster or more accurate way to identify a "successful, flourishing, or thriving condition" than by just calculating it in dollars and cents.

But does that mean the words "prosperity" and "money" are synonymous? To find an answer, we need to look at two types of people: one rich, the other poor. The first type, the rich, includes those we talked about in Chapter 1: lottery winners and inheritors of wealth. Because of the speed with which they attained their wealth, I call them the Instant Rich. Both varieties of Instant Rich have two things in common: (1) they either possess, or have the rights to, a great deal of money, and (2) they did little or nothing to earn it.

PROSPERITY AND THE INSTANT RICH

As I mentioned earlier, reliable statistics about these people are hard to come by, but we do have plenty of verified reports of how most lottery winners handle their sudden wealth. They take lavish vacations, buy luxury cars, give friends and family gifts of cash and generally spend themselves into holes they can never dig out of. As for the heirs of the wealthy, ask any attorney who's handled their money. You'll hear about alcoholism, drug addiction, chronic depression, family strife—all characteristics of people who feel unhappy, unfulfilled, worthless.

I'm not saying the suddenly wealthy are doomed to a life of waste and unhappiness. Some Instant Rich are able to increase their wealth, benefit society and build happy, productive lives. For these people, money and prosperity go hand in hand. I'm not talking about them.

I'm talking about people for whom money means only conflict and pain: lottery winners who have huge incomes, but spend so much they're always broke; scions who look rich, but feel poor because they fear that if the money ever ran out, they wouldn't know how to make more. These are the Instant Rich who have a lot of money, but no prosperity. They're not living in a "successful, flourishing, or thriving condition."

PROSPERITY AND THE PRODUCTIVE POOR

The second type of people are those we might call the Productive Poor. Let me tell you about a community of them that I came to know and admire.

When I started dating my wife, Wanda, in 1962, she lived in a predominantly Polish neighborhood on the near west side of Detroit. Back then, it was a genuine pleasure to drive through her neighborhood. The houses were always freshly painted or washed, the porches and sidewalks swept clean in summer and shoveled free of snow in winter. Since the houses were built on small, "postage-stamp" lots, there was little room for lawns and gardens. Nevertheless, the modest squares of grass were a deep green, lush and meticulously trimmed. The flowers bordering each house were bursting with color. The gardens were weeded and tended until they overflowed with huge cabbages, cucumbers, spinach and tomatoes. In front of most houses was a car—usually not new, but always washed, polished and in good running condition.

The people who lived in that neighborhood took pride not only in their property, but also in the way they dressed and groomed themselves. On Sundays, they put on their best outfits, scrubbed and dressed their children and walked to church, where they often gave more than they could afford. Most of the children attended privately funded Catholic schools, and many went on to college.

The neighborhood had an air of happiness and well-being about it. There was almost no crime. People were friendly, and visited with one another on their front porches. The divorce rate was nearly zero, and families stayed close together. When a young couple got married, they often rented a flat in the same block—or even the same house—as their parents. At Christmas, every house was decorated with hundreds of colored lights. Laughter and song could be heard from every living room.

To even the most casual observer, the people in Wanda's old neighborhood appeared prosperous in every way. They ate well, they bought what they needed, they paid cash for their houses, they lived virtually free of debt. Yet most of them were factory hands, doing semi-skilled labor in Detroit's auto plants, or in small machine shops.

But the neighborhood was no Disneyland. The work was hard and life was hard. Pay levels were low; lay-offs were common. Young children had to deliver newspapers in harsh weather and work at tough, menial jobs to help the family finances. There were no "days off." For adults and kids alike, vacation time did not mean relaxation. It was a time to catch up on chores, to scrub, paint and repair.

When I met Wanda, her father made his living with a broom and shovel in Ford's foundry; her mother cleaned offices in the Ford headquarters building at night. Like so many of their neighbors, they had been "poor" most of their lives. For years, they worked two jobs each to keep their five children fed, clothed and housed. But the food was nutritious, the clothing was clean and mended, the house was spotless and in good repair. By working, saving and spending wisely, the family always had enough of everything they really needed. They lived in a "successful, flourishing, and thriving condition." They were prosperous. Yet they had very little money—sometimes, none at all.

So there we have the two types of people: the Instant Rich, who have a lot of money, but no prosperity, and the Productive Poor, who have little money, but much prosperity. How can this be? Aren't money and prosperity supposed to be synonymous? If they're not the same thing, don't they at least go hand in hand?

No. Contrary to what you might have thought, *prosperity is not made of money*. And *money does not produce prosperity*.

Recently, we went back to the old neighborhood for a visit, and I got shocking proof of this truth. Wanda's mother still lives there. Her house and a few others still look the way they did back in the 1950s and 1960s. But most of the rest haven't been painted in years. The lawns are weedy and yellow, the gardens are gone. Junk cars rust away on the streets and in the backyards. On the main street, once-bustling stores are closed, boarded up and covered with graffiti.

Ironically, the people who live in the neighborhood now have more money (adjusted for inflation) than the Productive Poor whom they replaced. They too work in factories and stores. Many are on welfare, but ironically, they have incomes proportionately larger than Wanda's neighbors did when she was growing up.

Now, as then, the neighborhood is peopled by the poor. But whereas then the poor were prosperous, now they're not.

THE ESSENCE OF PROSPERITY

Studying these people teaches us that the essence of prosperity is *not* money. If it were, all people with money would be prosperous, and all those without it would *not* be. Yet as we've seen, this isn't so.

Actually, the essence of prosperity is *abundance*. The Random House Dictionary says abundance is "an extremely plentiful or over sufficient quantity or supply." The essence of abundance is *creation*. Abundance—and therefore prosperity—doesn't just happen. You can't win it or inherit it. You have to create it. Even the abundance of nature was created; not by man, of course, but it *was* created.

The Productive Poor in Wanda's old neighborhood had prosperity because they *created* it, they made it happen. Their prosperity came from something they carried around inside themselves, not from the money they carried in their pockets. What is the "something" that produced their prosperity? The answer is in the next chapter, but before we go on to it, we need to tie up one loose end.

DEFINING YOUR OWN PROSPERITY

Earlier I suggested that most people equate prosperity with money because it's easy to measure. But you've just seen that true prosperity *can't* be equated with money. So how do you know when you have it? And if you have it, how do you measure it?

To get a true picture of your prosperity, you must examine the relationships you've developed with the things you need and want. Some of the things you need, like food and clothing, are easy to account for. But other needs—love, satisfying relationships, rewarding work, a sense of security, self-esteem— can't be measured. A calculator will do you no good in figuring, for example, your pride in accomplishment. Yet if you had no pride in accomplishment, you could hardly call yourself prosperous. As for the things you *want*, again, some are easily measured—like the number of classic Mustangs in your car collection, or the number of vintage wines in your cellar. But suppose one of the things you want is simply to be happy. How do you measure that?

To define your own prosperity, you'll have to face the fact that much of it *can't* be measured, and indeed doesn't have to be. Henry Ward Beecher wrote, "It is the heart that makes a man rich. He is rich according to what he is, not according to what he has." If you're getting what you *need*—materially, emotionally, socially, spiritually—you're prosperous, and you know it. What's the point of being more accurate than that? Unless of course you're trying to show up somebody else. But when you do that you're not measuring your prosperity, you're measuring your ego.

Everyone has different needs, but the truth is, basic needs are relatively few, and fairly consistent from one person to another. The big variations come in the category of wants, or desires. There's no limit to how much you can want. No one needs a million dollars, but plenty of people want it. No one needs a million friends, either, but some people want that. You may have everything you *need* right now, but if you live to be a thousand years old, you'll probably never have everything you *want*. That's why it's absurd to say you won't consider yourself prosperous until you have everything you want. If so, you're headed not for prosperity, but frustration.

Instead, it's enough to say you're prosperous when you have what you really need, and the *means* or the *ability* to get what you want. When you define it in this way, prosperity can be yours *whether you have a lot of money or not*. If you have what you need and the means to get what you want, you're prosperous.

You may want to refine this definition and say, "Well, having the means to get what I want isn't enough. I won't consider myself prosperous until I'm actually moving in the direction of getting what I want—until I'm seeing some progress." If so, fine. In fact, that's very close to a definition of prosperity I found in another dictionary: "successful progress in any business or enterprise." When you state your definition in terms of progress or movement, it gives you a lot of room to be prosperous now, plus a lot more room in which to grow.

The important thing in these definitions is that you're not making your prosperity dependent on the amount of money you have. Because as we've already learned, money's got nothing to do with it. One of my clients, a wealthy financial planner, told me the most prosperous time in his life was a four-year period during which he lived in a Trappist monastery and had no money at all. Meanwhile, one of my distant relatives, who makes a six-figure income, lives in an upscale suburb and drives a new car every year, constantly complains about how poor he is. So prosperity doesn't depend on money. It depends on *you*.

THE ROLE OF MONEY IN YOUR FUTURE

Just because money isn't necessary for your prosperity doesn't mean you should forget about it. After all, as humans, we are physical beings with physical needs. Unless you plan to join a monastery, money will probably play an important role in your future. For one thing, it's the most efficient means for acquiring much of what you *need* in life, especially the material things. What's more, it may be the only way for you to get most of what you *want*.

I'm not saying you shouldn't concern yourself with money. What I'm saying is, for right now, don't be concerned about how you're going to *make* it. Instead, be concerned about learning the Secret to Permanent Prosperity. When you do, money will appear—because you, like the Productive Poor in that old Detroit neighborhood, will create it out of something that's inside you.

So, in this roundabout way, we have come to the place where your search for permanent prosperity begins. It begins not with what you have, but with who you are.

Born to Be Prosperous

"You already have everything that you need in order to experience a lifetime of prosperity."
—DR. WAYNE DYER

You can learn life's most valuable lesson about prosperity without ever going near a bank or brokerage house, without ever earning or investing a penny. Here's how. Go find a piece of vacant land. It can be as close as your own backyard. If you live in a city, you might have to walk a few blocks to find a suitable plot. Actually, for this lesson, just about any land will be "suitable." Barren, weedy, littered, it doesn't matter. In fact, the more forlorn this bit of dirt, the more dramatically will it teach you about prosperity.

First, clean it up. Remove the bottles and cans. Pull the weeds. Dig out and throw away the rocks, pieces of wood and other debris. Now, decide what you'd like to see growing there. Let's say you choose something easy, like beans. Go to a nursery or garden shop and ask the clerk what you have to do to make beans grow in this dirt. You'll probably be told you have to turn the soil to aerate it, add soil-builder or fertilizer, plant seeds a certain distance apart at a certain time of the year, then water and pull weeds regularly as your beans sprout and develop.

If you do all these things, you'll be rewarded with one of the most marvelous "miracles" of nature: an abundant crop of nutritious food, where just a few months earlier a barren weed lot had been. Your little plot of beans will be in a "successful, flourishing, or thriving condition." It will be prosperous.

But where did that prosperity come from? From you? Did *you* teach the soil how to turn seeds into beans? Of course not. *The soil already knew.* It had the ability to produce prosperity before you ever came along. All you did was set up the conditions necessary to make that prosperity happen. The "something" that creates prosperity is in the soil itself. I call that something "prosperity consciousness."

What makes the lesson of the soil so valuable is that it applies to people, too. As human beings, you, me, all of us are born with prosperity consciousness. As Wayne Dyer says, we already have everything we need to experience a lifetime of prosperity. The ingredients are already a part of us before we even start. Or as he goes on to say, "Truly you are not going to get 'it' all. You are 'it' already."

THE RIGHT, THE MEANS, THE ABILITY

When you were born, no matter what the circumstances, you had the *right* to be prosperous. Nowhere was it written that you must be poor, or unhappy, or deprived of anything you can aspire to. I know—some countries in the world have laws that aim to limit people's opportunity to become prosperous. But laws can't prevent anyone from leaving such countries if they earnestly want to, and finding a place where they can prosper. In fact, the more people's prosperity consciousness is suppressed, the more ardent becomes their desire to escape the suppression and create the lives they want.

In the past few years, the Berlin Wall has come down; the Soviet Union has disappeared; boatloads of people from Asia and Latin America have sailed to wherever they believed they could create prosperity for themselves. The tremendous motivation that caused these events is too powerful to have been learned. It could only be inborn.

The right to be prosperous is something you carry with you from the womb, and no one can take it away from you. You had it on the day you were born; you have it today. If you live in a country that gives you the opportunity to develop your prosperity consciousness, be grateful. For you, putting the Secret to work will be easier every step of the way.

Not only do you have the right to prosperity in your lifetime, you also have the *means* to achieve it. You have a brain—maybe not the smartest or fastest brain in the world, but if yours works well enough to read and understand this book, it's more than adequate to help you create your prosperity. Plenty of people have become prosperous with a lot less brainpower than you possess right now.

You also have health. It may not be perfect, but if your health permits you to employ any amount of sustained physical or mental effort, it also provides you the means to produce prosperity. Several years ago, I saw a television documentary about a man who was a quadriplegic, yet finished college, became a writer and made a nice living. He did it all with only his voice, and whatever movements he could make from the neck up.

So if you have a working brain and marginal health, you have the means. On top of that, you were born with *ability*: the ability to learn, the ability to communicate, the ability to create, the ability to find or produce an environment that supports your prosperity. All these abilities are as much a part of you as the hair that sprouts from under your skin. And you don't have to go out looking for these abilities. You brought them along when you arrived.

"SO WHY AIN'T I PROSPEROUS ALREADY?"

Good question. If prosperity is part of people's natural makeup, if it's imbued in everyone before they're born, we should all be prosperous, shouldn't we? By this same reasoning, all cultivated land should be overflowing with rich crops. But it's not. The natural prosperity of the soil can be thwarted by withholding water or nutrients, or allowing weeds and pests to intervene.

Just as farmers can sabotage their crops, people can and do sabotage their prosperity. Even though prosperity is a natural condition, it's short-circuited, impeded, stopped in any number of ways. We all know this, but we don't always know *why*. Given that prosperity is our birthright, why on earth would we *not* want to enjoy and increase it? In fact, why wouldn't we want to produce every enjoyable condition in our lives: good health, nurturing friendships, happy marriages?

I'm no psychologist, so I don't pretend to know what motivates people at the deepest levels. But it doesn't take a degree in psychology to observe that many people believe themselves unworthy of prosperity. Many others consider prosperity to be evil. Some are actually *afraid* of prosperity, believing that if they increase what they have, they'll lose their friends, or incur the jealousy of their relatives and coworkers.

If you're not already prosperous, any or all of these explanations could apply to you, and you may have to get to the root of them before you're able to fully open yourself to the prosperity you naturally deserve. How you go about doing that is beyond the scope of this small book. Here and now, it's enough for you to know that if prosperity has been eluding you, it's not because you don't have the right, the means or the ability to achieve it. All of that has been with you from the day you drew your first breath. It will all still be there on the day you discover why you've been stopping yourself. At this moment, don't concern yourself with why you "ain't prosperous already." Concern yourself with how you're going to develop your prosperity from now on.

POOR FARMERS MAKE POOR CROPS

As we learned from our weed lot, the soil has a "consciousness" that enables it to produce prosperity, and this consciousness exists independently of any outside source. However, if you want to grow crops, you have to use and develop that consciousness. It would be pointless for you to throw seeds onto hard, dry ground, then sit back and wait for results. If you did that, you'd be a poor farmer indeed, and not surprisingly, you'd produce a poor crop.

Yet that's exactly how most people approach their efforts at achieving prosperity. They buy lottery tickets. They gamble on horse races or football games. They scramble madly to make money before they know how to handle it, manage it, enjoy it or keep it. In the financial sense, they're poor farmers. No wonder they produce poor financial crops.

If you don't have the right prosperity consciousness—if you haven't properly prepared your financial "soil"—and money comes to you (as in a winning ticket or inheritance), you'll soon lose the money, or find that it makes you miserable.

On the other hand, if you develop your prosperity consciousness, it will produce a condition that creates abundance in your life. And the most exciting part is, it matters little what specific things you do to create that abundance. You can work, or play, or dance or sing. You can study, or not. You can put out a little effort, or a lot. It doesn't matter. The degree of your prosperity depends more on the state of your consciousness than it does on the specific action you take.

So far, we've learned:

- Prosperity doesn't come from money; rather, money comes from prosperity.

- Prosperity consciousness—the right, means and ability to produce prosperity—is an inborn part of you.
- To become prosperous, you must develop your prosperity consciousness, much as a farmer develops his soil.
- Once you develop your consciousness properly, prosperity will come—and it will hardly matter what you actually *do* to get it.

Knowing all this, to become prosperous, the only thing left for you to do is learn how to develop your prosperity consciousness. For that, all you need is the Secret, right? Yes, but first we have to answer just one more question, and it's important, so don't skip ahead.

Do You Really Want Prosperity?

"Prosperity depends more on wanting what you have than having what you want."
—GEOFFRY F. ABERT

Even though prosperity consciousness is a natural part of you, even though you were born to be prosperous in every way, your prosperity won't come to you automatically. Is this stating the obvious? Maybe, but I say it because many people (and we've all met some) believe that all they have to do is show up at work and eventually prosperity will come. Others think that since prosperity is their right, someone ought to come along and give it to them.

As we learned from driving through that old neighborhood in Detroit, if you want prosperity in your life, you can't sit around and wait for it to happen. You must create it. And before you can create it, you must truly, earnestly want it. Your desire must be clear. It must be intense. The clearer and more intense your desire, the more likely you are to make it real.

To know if you genuinely want prosperity, you need a complete mental picture of it. Then you must see yourself in that picture. If you can't imagine what prosperity is like, and if you can't imagine yourself experiencing it, your chances of creating it are small.

What does prosperity look like? Well, if you read movie magazines, or watch *Lifestyles of the Rich and Famous* on television, you might think that prosperity consists of sitting around on yachts sipping tall drinks, or jetting off to Cannes for the film festival, or popping over to Rodeo Drive in Beverly Hills for a facial and a massage.

While a few folks do live that way, the truth is, most prosperous people work, cook meals, raise their families, take care of their homes and do all the things everybody else does. The difference is, they do them at a different level—a different level of *consciousness*.

Several years ago, I took a seminar conducted by Marshall Thurber, a man who had become a millionaire while he was quite young. He said, "People are constantly asking me what it feels like to be a millionaire. Well, I'll show you, right now."

All of us in the seminar stirred with excitement; we were about to find out what it feels like to be rich. "Sit back in your chair and close your eyes," Marshall instructed. We did. "Now, take a deep breath and let it out," he said. We did that.

"There. That's what being a millionaire feels like."

Slowly, laughter spread through the room as we began to get his message: Being rich doesn't feel any different from anything else. Marshall went on to tell the story of what happened the day he first realized his personal net worth finally totaled over a million dollars.

"I went downstairs to breakfast, and my wife said, 'Marshall, take out the garbage.' I thought, 'Wait a minute, I'm a millionaire; millionaires shouldn't have to take out the garbage.' " Nevertheless, the garbage needed to be taken out, and since there was no one else there to do it, he did.

That garbage, he explained, taught him the best lesson he could have learned: Being rich doesn't exempt you from dealing with all the little things we must deal with in life. Fundamentally, rich people are just like everyone else. Or as W. C. Fields said, "A rich man is nothing but a poor man with money."

When your prosperity consciousness changes, in many aspects your life will stay the same. You'll still have problems to solve; you'll still get stuck in traffic; you'll still have good days and bad days. In short, you'll still be human. But in many important ways, your life will be dramatically different.

A PICTURE OF PROSPERITY

You'll live in a neighborhood that's better maintained and more attractive than the one you live in now. The homes will be larger. If you live in an apartment, the building will be more tastefully decorated, and the front door will be more likely to be attended. You'll drive to work in a car that's newer and runs more reliably than your current one. If you don't drive to work, you'll be more likely to take a cab than a bus or train.

You'll dress differently, of course. Your clothes will cost more, look better and last longer. You'll get your hair done more often, and because you'll be in a more prominent position, you'll probably keep it groomed more carefully. You'll still work, but your job will probably be less physical and more mental. You'll have more responsibility. There'll be more people asking you for advice and direction. More consequences will be attached to everything you do.

In your free time, you may be doing many of the same things you do these days, but with different people. When you're prosperous, you won't have as much in common with the folks you spend time with now. You'll want to be with people who look, dress and act more like you do.

You'll spend a lot of time thinking about money. Of course, you may do that already, but when you're prosperous, you'll have a lot more money to deal with, so you won't have to focus on making ends meet. As Johnny Carson said, "The thing money gives you is the freedom of not worrying about money." Instead of worrying, you'll be reading financial journals, considering investments, talking to advisors and generally trying to preserve, protect and increase your assets.

As we've seen, prosperity involves a lot more than money, so the nonfinancial aspects of a prosperous life are much different also. When you become completely prosperous, you'll put an end to relationships that don't support and nurture you. You'll distance yourself from the people in your life who have been draining you emotionally. Instead, you'll become closer to those who practice the prosperity principle of give-and-take. At first, it may bother you to lose touch with people you've known for a long time. But once you see how much they've been taking from you, you'll realize that losing those relationships is not costing you; in fact, it's paying off. Prosperous, nurturing people are more fun to be around anyway.

When you're prosperous, you'll waste less time on useless activities, like watching TV reruns and reading tabloids. You'll view life as being full of valuable opportunities and fascinating information, so you'll soon grow impatient with things that give you little or no value. When you're prosperous, you'll be healthier. Knowing you're a person of high worth, you'll be drawn to foods, exercise and health habits that enhance that worth. You'll need and want abundant energy to enable you to fully enjoy the abundance in the rest of your life.

Does all this sound radically different from the kind of life you live now? If so, get ready, because a new and fully prosperous life can be a challenge to handle.

MOVIN' ON UP

Some years ago, there was a television series called *The Jeffersons*. A weekly comedy, it presented the adventures of a New York couple from poor beginnings who built a successful chain of dry cleaning stores. They did so well in business, they were able to leave their working-class neighborhood and move to a plush high-rise on Manhattan's upper East Side. The theme music for this program, "Movin' On Up," encapsulated the tremendous changes the Jeffersons faced in their more prosperous environment. If you do what this book suggests and become prosperous, you, like the Jeffersons, will have to make the hundreds of adjustments your new environment will demand.

If you now dislike or resent people who are rich or prosperous, you'll have to change your attitude. In fact, you'd better start changing your opinion of such people right now. If not, you'll either sabotage your efforts to achieve prosperity (lest you become one of "them") or you'll hate yourself when you've achieved prosperity because you've joined the ranks of people you despise.

Finally—and this can be the hardest part—you'll have to endure the scorn of those who dislike prosperous people. You'll have to listen to politicians preaching about how we have to tax the rich more in order to have fairness in our society. You'll have to resign yourself to being regarded as "filthy rich," or a snob, or an exploiter of the poor—even if you're not all that rich, and not snobbish, and care deeply about the poor.

Don't underestimate the importance of this: Financial prosperity can produce difficulty in your life just as readily as it can produce satisfaction and well-being. Before you commit to creating prosperity for yourself, you have to accept this possibility. A friend of mine who is a psychotherapist told me she prefers to counsel people with a lot of money. Aside from the obvious advantage that they're able to pay more for her services, she'd rather deal with them because they already realize an important truth: *Money won't solve their problems.* People who don't have much money come in for counseling and say, "If my husband and I didn't have these financial pressures, we could get along better." Or, "When I get a better job, I'll have time to spend with my family." Or, "If I just had enough money, I'd jump on a plane and get away from all these troubles."

Once you've made money, and seen that marital problems don't magically disappear, that high-paying jobs take up just as much time as low-paying ones, that you take your problems with you wherever you go—then you'll know the limits of what financial success can do. That's why it's so important, when building your prosperity, to work on becoming prosperous in *every* area of your life. You must carefully maintain balance, because balance is what well-being is made of.

THE PRICE OF PROSPERITY

Before you start on your quest for prosperity, you must also realize that every opportunity to increase your wealth has its price. Several years ago, I learned this lesson in dramatic fashion. Having achieved a little recognition for my accomplishments, I found I was being asked to speak more often. If you've never done it, professional speaking looks like an easy way to make a lot of money. People will pay you thousands of dollars just to stand in a big room and move your mouth for a few minutes. What a deal!

I had made a few of these appearances, and was gearing up to get more, when I happened to encounter a fellow San Diegan who had already been a successful professional speaker for quite a few years. The encounter took place in the lobby of a hotel far from home. "Look at this," my friend said, excitedly showing me a magazine article with his byline on it. "This is just the beginning. I'm well on my way to becoming a writer."

"Why do you want to become a writer?" I asked. "Don't you make a lot more money, with a lot less grief, as a professional speaker?"

"Sure I do," he said. "But look where we are. This is where I live my life. In hotels, restaurants, airplanes. I have a son in elementary school, and since he's been born, I've seen him less than ten days out of every month. As a writer, I'll be able to stay home all the time if I want. I'll make less money, but so what?"

That stopped me. I realized that I too hate being away a lot, that my home life is more important to me than all the money I could make on the road. I also realized that as a writer, I *already had* what my friend was so earnestly trying to achieve. So I stopped looking for speaking engagements (though I still accept the occasional offer, especially if it's close to home). I know this has cost me a lot of money over the years. I know I'm not as prosperous, financially, as I would have been if I'd kept up the speaking. But it's a level of wealth I was willing to give up in order to get another kind of prosperity. And while I've often wondered what it would have been like to have all that extra money, I've never regretted passing on it.

Once you learn and begin using the Secret to Permanent Prosperity, you'll see there's no limit to the amount of prosperity you can create in every area of your life. At that point, your biggest decision will be whether or not you want it. Right now, it's enough for you to know that the effects of prosperity are not necessarily all desirable and that prosperity won't necessarily bring you bliss. Often it brings just the opposite.

Now, after all that, do you still want prosperity? Good. Here's the Secret.

A Simple Secret

"I have always noticed that the man who gives the most for the money, gets the most business."
—VASH YOUNG

In the 1950s and 1960s, American auto companies were the most prosperous in the world. They virtually owned the market. European and Japanese industry, having been bombed to near oblivion during World War II, could not compete. Yet by the early 1970s, the situation had changed dramatically. Japanese cars—especially the small, economical models—were selling briskly. By the 1980s, American autos had lost a sizable chunk of their market share, and manufacturers were starting to close plants to cut costs. Checker Motors (the taxicab maker) closed down, American Motors Corporation was bought out, and the United States was left with only its Big Three. Meanwhile, Japanese automakers, which were reaching the limits of their domestic production capacity, began buying and building auto plants in the United States. At one point, no fewer than ten Japanese manufacturers were selling vehicles in the American market.

Obviously this turnabout was a very complicated phenomenon, and many factors, political as well as economic, contributed to it. I don't want to risk oversimplifying what happened, yet I can't help asking some obvious questions.

Weren't the Japanese and the Americans operating in the same industry? Weren't they selling in the same markets? Weren't the same world economic conditions affecting each? Yet the Japanese manufacturers grew steadily more prosperous while the Americans became less so. Why?

An auto industry analyst could probably spend hours responding to the last question, but I submit a simple answer: Because the Japanese were building better cars and selling them at lower prices. While owners of Pontiacs and Chryslers were taking them in for one recall repair after another, Honda and Toyota owners were happily running up hundreds of thousands of trouble-free miles. Shoppers for American cars were being advised not to buy any built on Mondays or Fridays because on those days, the assembly line workers were more likely to be absent or hung over. At the same time, shoppers for Japanese cars were being shown how well imports were doing in customer-satisfaction surveys.

The ultimate difference between the two groups of manufacturers was this: The Japanese were delivering more *value*, so they got more business; the Americans stopped delivering value, so they got less business. As a consumer, if you can get a better product for a price that's about the same or lower than a competing product, you buy it. You come away feeling you've gotten a better *value*. Even if you have a strong sentimental attachment to the product that's not a good value—even if you feel it's your patriotic duty to buy the product—in the end, *value* determines what you'll buy.

In this example lies a powerful truth: *You create prosperity by delivering value.*

But this is only part of the story. Notice also that the Japanese companies delivering this value were operating profitably. In other words, they accepted value in return. By accepting a profitable level of compensation, they were able to replenish their supplies of materials, upgrade their plants, add production capacity and thus create more value.

When you put these two ideas together, you have part of our prosperity secret. In one sentence, it's this: *To be prosperous, you must deliver value, and accept value in return.* The secret to prosperity is based on circulation, give-and-take, outflow and inflow, a cycle of value provided and value received.

If you give too little and take too much in return, you're not delivering value, and eventually the market will stop coming to you. On the other hand, if you give too much and take too little in return, sooner or later you'll lose your ability to create more. An auto manufacturer that can only deliver value by operating unprofitably will eventually go broke. Taking too much or giving too much cuts off the circulation, and when that happens, prosperity is destroyed.

MAKING PROSPERITY PERMANENT

Again, this is the secret to prosperity: To be prosperous, you must deliver value and accept value in return. But it's *still* not the whole story. Many have used this Secret to create prosperity, only to lose it in a short time, or hang on to it for a few years, then let it slip away.

Too many self-help and get-rich books tell you how to make money, build a fortune, create prosperity—but they end right there, assuming that's all you need to know. In my view, it's just as important—maybe even more so—to know how to make prosperity *permanent*, to make it a part of your life until your life is over. When you can do that, *then* you've got prosperity worth working for.

Fortunately, once you've grasped the concept of creating prosperity, making it permanent is relatively simple. Not only must you deliver and accept value, but you must keep on doing it for as long as you want your prosperity to last. If you want your prosperity to last as long as you live, that's how long you need to keep creating it.

When we put all these ideas together, we get the Secret to Permanent Prosperity:

> *To be prosperous, you must deliver value and accept value in return; to be permanently prosperous, you must continue delivering and accepting value for the rest of your life.*

CREATING AND DELIVERING VALUE

Now that we've learned the entire Secret, let's look at it one piece at a time. Prosperity starts when you create value. Going back to our garden analogy, when you improve the soil, you add value to it. The soil responds by giving you value in return. You put in effort, fertilizer, seeds and water; you get back beans. If it's beans you want, then you've gotten the value you were hoping for.

If it's money you want, then you must create value for *people*, because only people can give you money. If you grow beans, but what you really want is money, then you must find people who value beans. When you deliver beans to such people, and they appreciate the beans' value, they'll give you money in return. By growing beans, *you've created value*. By delivering the beans to people and accepting money in return, *you've created prosperity*.

Before we get too deeply into the subject of money, remember that the rules of prosperity apply to every aspect of life. You can create abundant good health, rewarding relationships, well-being, whatever prosperity means to you, by using the same principles that apply to money. In my examples, I talk about money because it's easy to measure and it's a common prosperity goal for many people.

If you, like so many others, want to enhance your prosperity by making more money, you must increase the value of what you provide to whoever pays you. To get more money for your beans, you must produce better beans—or do something that will make them worth more to the bean buyer.

For people in business for themselves, or direct sales, increasing value is a straightforward proposition: Improve your product and more people will buy it. Boost your sales figures and commissions will increase. But suppose you work in a salaried job where you're paid for the time you spend on duty, such as municipal employment. How can you create value, let's say, as a clerk in the office that issues dog licenses? Not as clear-cut, but it can be done.

To start with, you can create value by doing your job exceptionally well. You're not just paid to *be* there; you're paid to *do* something. You can become the most courteous, most punctual, most efficient dog-license clerk your city has ever known. Next, you can do more than you're being paid for. You can come in a few minutes early to straighten up, brew coffee, organize the files—do the little things that make everyone's work easier and more pleasant. You can also devise new, more cost-effective ways to get your job done.

I once made these suggestions to someone employed by a county government, and he scoffed. "You just don't understand," he said. "That stuff doesn't apply in the public sector. I get paid the same amount no matter how hard I work. Promotions are given according to seniority. If I do more than I'm paid for, the union will be all over me."

Would it surprise you to learn this man has been in the same job for many years? But suppose he's right. Suppose some employers don't directly reward greater effort with greater pay. Can an employee in such a situation create prosperity anyway?

Of course, and here's how it happens. When you become known as the best, most courteous, most punctual, most efficient dog-license clerk your city has ever known, word gets around. People talk. There isn't a supervisor alive—in government, business or anywhere else—who isn't looking for that kind of worker. And when that supervisor hears about you, he or she will start recruiting you.

Maybe in your department, promotions come only with seniority. But if you move to another department, or get a new job classification, you may jump several salary levels overnight. And don't say it doesn't happen. It happens every day, even in the most rigidly structured organizations. To prove this for yourself, find a department whose top person is relatively young, and ask by what route he or she made it to that position. I'll bet not one in ten got there by simply doing the minimum amount of work and waiting for promotions. I'll also bet a fair number of them got to the top by a route not shown on any organizational chart.

You are literally surrounded by opportunities to create value. These golden opportunities are everywhere, and they're popping up all the time. To become prosperous, you must keep your eyes open for them, and take advantage when they come along. But don't make the mistake of keeping your accomplishments a secret. When you do create value, make sure it's noticed—not by bragging or selfishly clamoring for attention, but by making sure the message gets to people who are in a position to return value to you. If you create value and no one knows about it, if you give more and don't get more in return, you're not using the Secret. Instead of becoming prosperous, you're becoming a victim. We've all met such victims at one time or another—people who labor for years, unappreciated, unrewarded, unfulfilled. We may feel sorry for them, but the truth is, they're unrewarded because they haven't asked for the rewards they deserve. They haven't communicated the value of what they create to people who are in a position to properly reward that value.

But such people are the exception. In real life, when someone is really good, it doesn't stay a secret for long. The marketplace—every marketplace—is looking for value, and when value is spotted, it gets snapped up. My friend Hans is a perfect example of this phenomenon.

Hans had spent a number of years in real estate, usually working for himself, and usually in the mortgage lending part of the business. He had been mildly successful, but it bothered him that he had no real credentials. He had never worked for a large company, and thus had never demonstrated an ability to, in his words, "play with the big boys."

To get the credentials he needed, he took a job as a regional loan manager with a major Southern California bank, at a salary of $30,000 per year. Hans immediately made his presence felt. He simplified loan application procedures, hired new salespeople, streamlined operations—and quickly had his region producing more than ever before. Soon, his was the top region in the state.

People noticed. Real estate brokers, other mortgage brokers, employees of other banks—all of them started talking about how Hans was transforming his bank. A man named Arnold, who owned a real estate brokerage, had several dealings with Hans, and was impressed with his ability to get things done. Arnold was thinking of opening his own mortgage company, and decided Hans would be the right person to run it. So he offered Hans the job—at $40,000 per year. Feeling he didn't have all the experience he needed as yet, Hans turned it down.

At the time, he didn't know that Arnold was the type of person who would not take no for an answer. He offered Hans $50,000. Hans turned it down. A few months later, he offered $60,000. This time, Hans thought it over a long while before turning it down. When the ante got to $75,000 plus a piece of the profits, Hans said, "I'll talk to the bank. If they match your offer, I'll stay. If they don't, I'll move."

A few days later, Hans went to see his boss, a high-ranking bank executive. "How am I doing?" he asked.

"Hans, we're delighted with your performance. Since you've come on board, not only is your region setting records every month, but by following your example the other regions are doing better too. We're thinking of promoting you. Of course, the promotion would be a title only, not a raise."

"No raise, huh?" Hans said. "Would it be safe to say the bank's making more money because of me?"

"Oh yes, a great deal more. You know that."

"How much? Hundreds of thousands of dollars per year?"

"Easily."

"Well, if the bank's making hundreds of thousands more because of my efforts, why wouldn't you pay me more?"

"Because in our organization, Hans, the next step does not involve a raise. It involves a title."

"But I don't want a title. I'd prefer more money."

"I'm sorry, Hans, I just can't give it to you."

"Someone can," Hans said, and described Arnold's offer.

Hans's boss was stricken. He was about to lose the best regional loan manager he'd ever had. "Let me see what I can do," he replied.

The next day, Hans got the word. The bank would promote him two steps and give him a raise to $35,000. Hans could barely keep from laughing in his boss's face. He went to work for Arnold, and to no one's surprise, has built the company into one of the most successful in California. Last year, he made over $300,000. The bank, which tried to accept greatly increased value from Hans without delivering greatly increased value in return, was bought out by a larger bank, and no longer exists.

Hans created value, he delivered value, he let his value be known. If you do those things, the marketplace will fall all over itself to make you prosperous. Don't just take my word for it; try it and see.

If to you prosperity means something other than money, you can achieve it in the same way: by creating value. If you want to have lots of friends, give something of value to people: your time, attention, assistance, caring. If want abundant health, give your body the value of wholesome food, regular exercise, adequate rest. Whatever you give, you get back in abundance. Remember, the essence of prosperity is abundance, and the essence of abundance is creation.

HOW TO BE PROSPEROUS FOR THE REST OF YOUR LIFE

If you want to live successfully, just becoming prosperous isn't enough. You have to make that prosperity a permanent part of your life. Some years ago, a financial publication asked me to do an article about athletes, models and rock musicians—relatively young people who earned huge amounts of money in a few years. The magazine was interested in finding out how they invested that money, so I interviewed financial managers, business agents and investment advisors who had worked with the talented, rich and famous. I found out most of these superstars were broke within a few years of retirement. They had discovered how to create prosperity, but not how to live with it.

"The first mistake they make," one agent told me, "is they think their glory years will last forever. So they make a million dollars a year and spend a million and a half. By the time they retire—at age thirty-something—they're too deep in debt to ever get out."

A financial advisor told me about the second most common mistake: bad investments. "Athletes, musicians, models, actors—these are all people with tremendous ability who are hopelessly naive about money. So they fall for every scam that comes along. An old college buddy tells them about a great investment growing avocados in Australia, and they jump in, sign a bunch of documents, and in a few years, have to pay millions just to get out. It's pitiful."

These are people who did not learn how to make

their prosperity permanent. Yet if they had studied a little, and taken some sound advice, they could have been living in luxury for the rest of their lives, rather than trying to extend their fading careers with risky surgery just to keep from losing everything.

To be permanently prosperous, you must *continue* to deliver value to people, and accept value in return.

You can deliver value without working. After your working years are done, you can invest your savings, or at the very least, leave it in the bank. Your investment capital, when used to buy stocks, will help people build businesses, manufacture products, create value. They'll reward you with dividends, and with increased market values in your stocks. If you deposit your money in the bank, you make it available for people to borrow in the form of mortgages, car loans, student loans—all the things they need to finance their dreams. The interest they pay not only supports the bank, it supports you. As a bank depositor, you can deliver and receive value for the rest of your life—and you don't have to work another minute.

If you're reaching the end of your earning years, and your investment capital isn't enough to live on, you can still create permanent prosperity. You can deliver value by teaching and helping younger people to do their jobs more effectively, so *they* in turn can create more value in the marketplace. You can give advice and direction—and receive money, gifts or favors in return.

The point is, as long as you're alive, you have the capacity to create value for people. As long as you can figure out a way to deliver value, you can find people who will reward you for it. As long as you continue being rewarded for creating value, you'll continue being prosperous. And that's the Secret to Permanent Prosperity.

The Road to Prosperity Is Paved With Value

"A thing has intrinsic value if its essence is in demand because of its essential contribution to some human purpose."

—VALIDIVAR

If you want to learn an important lesson about prosperity, conduct a little research on your own. I guarantee it will be fun—and eye-opening.

When you encounter someone whom you consider prosperous, ask if he or she came to be so by choice, rather than by luck or accident. Keep asking people until you feel you've gotten a representative sampling. I predict that overwhelmingly, they'll say it was a matter of choice. Few, if any, of your respondents will say they lucked into their prosperous circumstances.

Then ask people who are *not* prosperous if they got where they are by choice. I predict most of them will attribute their situation to something outside themselves, something they could not control: bad luck, disadvantaged background, lack of opportunity. Convinced external forces control them, they'll argue vehemently that the life they're living is not the life they chose.

In the years I've been writing self-help books, I've been on radio talk shows dozens of times, and taken hundreds of calls from people who insist their lack of prosperity is not their fault, and certainly not their choice.

When I hear that, I don't disagree. I just say, "All right, life has dealt you some bad hands. But let's forget about the past. Right now, this minute, do you get to choose what you'll do next?"

Some say yes, others cling to their story and insist they don't have a choice.

I keep trying. "When you end this phone conversation, can you choose whether you'll go to bed, turn on the TV or read a book?"

Well, yes, they admit.

"Of those three choices, which is most likely to contribute more to your future well-being?"

Reading a book, most of them reply.

"Then at this very moment, you face a choice that can make a difference in your life, start you on the road to something better or keep you traveling the road you're on. Which will it be?"

What follows is usually what the radio people call "dead air."

Here's the point: Prosperity is a matter of *choice*. It always has been. If you haven't recognized it before, that's regrettable; you've missed a lot. But it's not too late, because you still have a choice. Now, five minutes from now, tonight, tomorrow, next week. Every moment brings new choices, new opportunities to decide which way your life will go. You can start creating your prosperity anytime, no matter what your current circumstances, no matter what's happened in the past. Just ask anyone who's done it.

When you first choose to alter your circumstances and become prosperous, you'll be making your life more difficult. Without question, it's harder to read a book than it is to watch TV or go to bed. That's just the way life is.

In the movie *A League of Their Own*, Geena Davis, playing the role of the star catcher on history's first all-female professional baseball team, decides to quit just before the championship series. Tom Hanks, playing the part of her manager, Jimmy Dugan, asks why.

"I didn't know it would be this hard," she replies.

"Of course it's hard," he says. "If it wasn't hard, everyone would do it. It's the *hard* that makes it great."

This bit of Hollywood wisdom applies to your prosperity as readily as to any aspect of life. If it wasn't hard to create prosperity, everyone would do it. In the beginning, at least, expect it to be difficult, much more so than it would be if you just left things as they are.

After a while, things change. What at first took real effort and discipline in time becomes routine. The hard things get easier. The more prosperous you become, the less effort is required to stay that way.

Ironic, isn't it? When you *don't* choose to become prosperous, at first it's easy, but later it gets harder. When you *do* choose to become prosperous, it starts out hard, but gets easier as you go. Don't be intimidated by the initial difficulty. Expect it, welcome it, look beyond it. In the immortal words of Jimmy Dugan, "It's the *hard* that makes it great."

THE STEPS TO YOUR PROSPERITY

Okay, you've been raising your prosperity consciousness, you've come to fully understand the Secret and you know the path you've chosen is going to be hard, at least in the beginning. You're ready to begin anyway. What's the first step?

The first step doesn't involve physical movement; it's all mental. First, you must accept that no one owes you anything. Whatever you get in life, you have to create. Whether it's a job, an education, a relationship, or a business, you can't wait for anyone to give it to you, for help to come along. If you've just been hanging around, marking time, hoping to catch a break, forget it. Accept reality: You have to make your own breaks.

We've already learned that the essence of prosperity is abundance and the essence of abundance is creation. You must *create* in order to prosper, and you don't create by waiting around for something to happen. You create by reaching down inside yourself and finding something that has value, something you can deliver to people that will *serve* them in some way.

The second step, then, is to create value out of what you know, or what you can do or who you are. If you don't *know* anything that can be of value to people, you can learn. If you don't *do* anything people will pay for, you can develop a skill, or devise a service of some kind. If all you have is your own personality, your own *self* to share, you can create value by offering that.

This ability you have—to create value—is a tremendous opportunity. It's not limited by any external factor. You can create and deliver value in any place, in any way, in any economic environment.

Value can be created in any place. In 1988, Wanda and I traveled to Poland to visit relatives and to learn about our Polish heritage. At the time, Poland was still a Communist country, and private enterprise was not supposed to exist. Over 95 percent of the Polish people are devout Catholics, yet officially, the country was atheist. So the Catholic Church there suffered from governmental repression and severe financial hardship.

Our tour stopped in a small town whose main attraction was a large, extremely ornate cathedral built hundreds of years ago by the peasants of the area. We stopped in that town because the priest, who knew and loved this old cathedral, spoke English. He was thus able to act as a guide for the many tourists who came through, most of whom were non-Polish-speaking Americans. Grateful for the priest's fascinating stream of facts and anecdotes about the great Gothic building, the tourists generously "donated" by filling a collection basket with precious American dollars.

Giving those little tours enabled the priest to generate revenue for his beloved cathedral, keep it in good repair and help the people of his parish to boot. Mind you, this was in a country whose strong central government frowned on both entrepreneurship and religion.

Value can be created in any way. When I first started in the advertising business in 1969, I worked for a man named Ed, who loved to tell the story of how he made money as a boy during the Depression. Ed's family lived near a golf course and Ed, who was fascinated by the game, would walk over and watch people playing. He would stand at the fence for hours, and got a particular kick whenever someone hit a ball into the water hazard. The players would moan and curse, and most would try to fish the ball out. But the little artificial lake was too deep, and usually they just gave up, took a penalty and played another ball.

Young Ed saw an opportunity. He invented a device that enabled him to get the golf balls from the deepest part of the water hazard, and in the evenings, after the playing stopped, he would hop the fence and retrieve the balls. Having been used and then soaked awhile, the balls were scuffed and discolored. Ed devised a way to paint them to look white as new. Then he'd go back to his spot at the fence, and when someone hit a ball into the hazard he'd say, "Hey Mister. Wanna buy another ball? Half the price of a new one." And buy it they did. In this way, Ed developed a fondness for golf and for entrepreneurship, both of which he loves to this day. (He's in his seventies now and is still an avid golfer and active businessman.) Remember, Ed's introduction to prosperity took place during the Great Depression, arguably the worst economic period in American history.

Value can be created in any economic environment. Speaking of the Great Depression, in 1979 I did an article for a stockbrokers' magazine about the fiftieth anniversary of the 1929 stock market crash, which is generally acknowledged to be the event that triggered the Depression. I was privileged to interview several people who had been involved in the crash, both as brokers and as investors.

One of the former investors was a man named Cohen, who in 1929 lived in New York and ran a small restaurant supply company. Mr. Cohen had possessed the foresight to pull his money out of the stock market before the crash. ("I knew it couldn't go up *forever*," he explained.) Once the crash came, he found himself with a little cash, while most people had none. Mr. Cohen was not then rich, but he soon would be.

During the ensuing Depression, a great number of apartment buildings went into foreclosure because their owners had borrowed against their equity to put money into the stock market. Suddenly banks all over town found themselves taking title to hundreds of apartment buildings they didn't want.

One day, Mr. Cohen was visiting his banker, who was lamenting the situation. "We've got all these apartment buildings, with no one to run them," he said. "If I could just find someone with a little cash for a down payment, someone who could sign a note and keep these buildings going, I'd just about *give* him the title."

Mr. Cohen volunteered to be that someone. "I bought so many buildings, I can't tell you," he recalled, "some of them for as little down as one dollar per unit. A hundred units, a hundred dollars down. It was a big job, managing them, keeping them up. But in the end it was worth it." By the time the Depression was over, Mr. Cohen had become a rich man.

Value can be created for any particular group. Nowadays, many people live alone and keep pets for companionship. The problem is, when you live alone and travel a lot, you have to find someone to care for your pet. There are kennels, of course, but many animals can't endure the stress of being pulled out of their home and kept in a cage for days at a time. A pet owner can always ask a friendly neighbor to stop by, but after a while, this can be an imposition.

In marketing terms, these pet owners constitute a "niche"—a small part of a larger market, a segment that has special needs. Astute entrepreneurs have identified this niche and are offering "pet-sitting" services; for a reasonable fee, they will come into your home, feed your pets, play with them, clean up after them and make sure they're happy and healthy.

What's the common thread running through these examples?

- The Polish priest *created value* for tourists in an unlikely place.
- Young Ed *created value* for golfers in an original way.
- Mr. Cohen *created value* for bankers and apartment dwellers during depressed economic times.
- The pet-sitters are *creating value* for a forgotten little segment of the pet-owner market.

Every one of these people developed prosperity by creating value—in most cases, out of nothing . . . nothing but their knowledge, their energy or their desire to serve. Opportunities to create value are all around you, right now. It doesn't matter where you live, how much money you have or what shape the economy's in. The only critical factor that determines whether you'll create value or not is *you*. Everything else, and I mean *everything* else, is incidental.

Developing Your Prosperity Consciousness

"The feeling must come first. If you actually feel rich, if you have a deep inner conviction that you will always have all that you need, it will be so."
—DONALD CURTIS

You may remember my saying earlier that most people equate prosperity with money because it's easy to measure. For the same reason, I'm going to suggest that in the beginning, you focus on developing your prosperity consciousness as a way of building your *material wealth*, rather than other kinds of abundance. Not that the nonmaterial things aren't just as important—in fact, many are more so. It's just that with money, you'll see results more easily and dramatically. You'll learn the lessons of prosperity more quickly, and you'll more readily apply them to the nonmaterial aspects of your life. Also, you'll be able to accurately measure your progress.

Whenever you're making a change, it's better to choose the path that holds the highest potential for success—because if you succeed early and often, you immediately begin reinforcing your new success pattern; you get a good, fast start, and a good start can be half the journey.

That being said, let's go back to something else we learned early on: Prosperity and money are not the same thing. Prosperity can *include* money, and usually *involves* money, but it does not automatically result when money appears, as so many lottery winners have already learned. Therefore, it's pointless for you to try to create prosperity in your life simply by making more money.

Money is outside yourself; prosperity is within. Money comes from other people; prosperity comes from *you*. Develop your prosperity consciousness, and money will come, in abundance. Turn your soil, aerate it, fertilize it, water it, plant seeds, tend your garden— and the crops will come, in abundance. Rather than trying to create prosperity by making more money, do what you need to do to become more prosperous, *within yourself*.

If you've never experienced prosperity, you probably don't know what it feels like. Even though you're born with prosperity consciousness, you may not recognize it within yourself. How do you develop something you've never felt and may not even recognize? Here's one way to go about it.

THE MAGIC OF MODELING

For many years, the Soviet Union produced the best Olympic athletes and ballet dancers in the world. They did it by employing a technique called "modeling" or "imaging." It worked like this: The government conducted nationwide auditions, searching for those young people who had the most raw talent and desire to excel as athletes or dancers. When these outstanding individuals were selected, they were assigned to live and study with a master in their field. The young person was told to imitate everything the master did—everything, not just work or exercise routines. In this way, the apprentice would form the same habits and use the same techniques the master had developed in becoming great. The "magic" of this method was evident in the results: Often the protégé reached greater heights of achievement than the mentor had. The inborn talent, the inherent "consciousness" of the beginner, when cultivated and developed by the proven techniques of the experienced one, produced a level of athletic "prosperity" above that which existed before.

APPLYING THE TECHNIQUE IN YOUR LIFE

You can use this technique to develop your prosperity consciousness, no matter at what level you now find yourself. Start by choosing an appropriate model or models. Observe people closely, especially those who have an air of prosperity about them—in other words, people who seem to be operating at the level you aspire to. What is it about them that looks prosperous? How do they act and speak? What kind of attitude do they project? How do they dress? How do they take care of their hair, complexion, fingernails, makeup? Are their clothes clean and pressed? Are their shoes shined?

At work, find an excuse to go to the floor or section where the executives work. Notice how the people there keep their desks, meeting rooms and conference areas. For the most part, are the work spaces cleaner and more organized than those of the lower-paid workers? Do the desktops of the highest-ranking people give you the impression of calm, control and self-assurance, the feeling that these people know what they're doing?

Visit a prosperous-looking area in your town. Remember, it doesn't have to be a neighborhood in which the people make a lot of money. As we've seen, the Productive Poor can exude as much prosperity as the materially wealthy.

Notice the way the people who live in that area take care of things. Observe how the lawns, shrubs and flowers are maintained. Do you see paint peeling or shutters falling off? Is there garbage spilling out of the trash cans, or strewn all over the sidewalk? Check out the prosperous people's cars. Are they kept clean and shiny? Can you see any fenders bashed in or bumpers held on with wire? Any coat hangers serving as radio antennas?

Once you've thoroughly observed and analyzed the appearance and activities of prosperous people, look at these elements in yourself, and compare.

Is your hair cut, washed and styled, or is it flying off in several directions? Does it have the greasy look of hair that's not been shampooed in several days?

Look at your hands. Are they clean? Is there dirt under your fingernails? Are the nails trimmed and filed, or are they ragged and bitten down?

What about your clothes? I realize they may not be the highest quality, but are they clean and pressed? Are they torn, even a little? Do you have any buttons missing? The style may not be the latest, but do the colors match? Or does it look like you got up this morning and just threw on whatever you saw first? Are your shoes shined, or are they scuffed and cracked? Are the heels worn down?

Look around your work area. You can keep a clean, well-organized space no matter where you work. I once worked in a machine shop, and noticed that the best, highest-paid operators always kept their area swept, their machines oiled and their materials neatly stacked and organized. Other guys doing the same type of work seemed always to be standing ankle-deep in metal shavings, while piles of parts spilled all around them. This second type were never asked to work much overtime, or do special jobs offering extra pay.

Whether you work in an office or shop, compare your work space to the executive areas you saw before. What message are you communicating to those who enter your space? Are you saying this person is competent, in control, getting things done? Or are you saying this person can't handle the job?

Go through the same exercise with the place you live and the car you drive. Just look at them, and with the eye of a disinterested observer, see what your home and car say about you. If you really want to learn about yourself, ask someone else to do the exercise for you. Choose a person whom you know and trust, someone you feel would be genuinely interested in helping, not just criticizing. Ask something like, "Fred, you've been my friend for a lot of years. When you look at my car, what do you see? If you didn't know me, and saw my car

on the street, what would you think of the owner?"
Fred's answers might surprise you.

WORK A MIRACLE WITH YOUR CAR

Since cars are so important in our society, I'd like
to spend a few minutes talking about them specifi-
cally. First, I realize that, in your present situation,
you may not be able to drive a car that will automatically impress people. If all you can afford is your
'74 Plymouth, so be it. But because your car is old,
and the odometer has gone back to zero a few times,
doesn't mean it has to look like the owner is tottering
on the brink of financial ruin.

If a '74 Plymouth is the best you can do, make
it the most prosperous-looking '74 Plymouth on the
road. Wash it, wax it—use finish-restorer if you have
to, but make sure it has a good shine. Shampoo the
interior, from headliner to floor. If there are any
broken knobs or handles, go to a junk yard and
find replacements.

Next, fix it up. If you don't have the money to
hire a mechanic, find a friend or relative who's handy
with cars. Offer to cook dinner, do laundry, clean
house, whatever it takes to compensate him or her
for putting your car into good running condition.
Make sure everything works, not just the engine.
Windshield wipers, radio, heater—all of these are
helpful conveniences when they work right, mad-
dening annoyances when they don't.

When you've done all that, when you've gotten
your car into the best shape it can possibly be, given
its age and past abuse, go for a drive. Notice how

different you feel—not just about the car, but about yourself. Before, you may have felt anxiety when you had to be somewhere and you hopped into that car, knowing it might quit on the way. Now, you can get behind the wheel feeling calm and confident, knowing you're going to get there. You can think about the meeting you're headed for, rather than making excuses for being late, or not showing at all.

Before, you may have felt embarrassed when you had to drive someone. You may have been concerned they'd think of you as a loser because of the rattle-trap you drove. Now you can be proud to give someone a lift. You can even secretly imagine they're thinking of you as being an affluent aficionado of vintage cars. Who knows—they might be.

The new feelings you're experiencing—the calm, the confidence, the pride—are the result of an increase in your prosperity consciousness. By raising the consciousness level of your car, you have actually raised the level of your own consciousness. You've caused an internal shift to occur, a shift that has you operating on a higher wavelength. How much did this little miracle cost? For the wash and wax, a few dollars. For the mechanical work, maybe a few hundred. Of course, there was your own time and effort. But of all the things you could have done to launch yourself on the road to prosperity, would any of them have produced more dramatic results in less time?

If you don't have a car, do the same kind of makeover on your apartment, or anything else that's a big part of your life. When you've completed, you'll have taken an important first step to developing your prosperity consciousness. You will have experienced what prosperity feels like. And you'll be well on your way.

Changing One Thing Changes Everything

"Sow an act, reap a habit; sow a habit, reap a character; sow a character, reap a destiny."
—GEORGE DANA BOARDMAN

Have you ever tried to move one piece of furniture in a fully furnished room? Let's say it's a chair, sitting in a spot where you constantly bump into it. The room would be fine, you think, if only that chair were somewhere else. So you move it.

The painting that was above the chair looks strange with nothing below it, so you move a table there. Now the rocker that was next to the table has no place for you to put a drink while you're sitting in it, so you have to move another table—or move the rocker. Doing that creates another empty space you have to fill by rearranging some of the bigger pieces. Before you know it, you've redone the whole room— all because of that one little chair.

Your life works the same way. It's fully furnished, with work, relationships, leisure activities, chores, family obligations—all the things that gobble up your time and attention. When you change one thing in your life, sometimes even a minor thing, it changes everything else.

About twelve years ago, my wife started jogging with some friends after work. At the time, I smoked cigarettes and wasn't too interested in any activity that didn't involve sitting down for long periods. But I did enjoy spending time with her, and I missed having her come right home from work so we could be together.

In her typically diplomatic way, Wanda began to suggest that I join the little jogging group. "It feels great to get out in the fresh air and move your large muscles at the end of the day," she would say. "We only run about twenty minutes; you'd hardly break a sweat." Eventually, she talked me into it. I started jogging a half mile, then a mile, then two. She was right; I did enjoy the fresh air, the exercise and the camaraderie with the other runners.

"This is great," I thought. "I can keep smoking, keep on living my sedentary life, and the jogging will make me feel less guilty about it." I soon found out otherwise.

After we'd been running two miles for a week or so, the rest of the group began stretching it to two and a half, then three. Meanwhile, I was stuck at two miles. No matter how often I ran, I couldn't get past that distance. It soon became obvious the cigarettes were holding me back. I didn't want to give up the jogging; I was enjoying it too much. But having tried to quit smoking literally hundreds of times in over twenty years, I was sure I couldn't. What was I to do?

Well, my desire to break through the two-mile

barrier became so strong, I did quit smoking. And to my surprise, I found quitting easier than it had ever been before. Suddenly food started to taste better, so I began putting on pounds. To keep my weight down, I changed my diet to foods lower in fat and sugar. This led to a greater awareness, at first of nutrition, and later of health in general. Today, a dozen years later, I still don't smoke, exercise has become an integral part of my life, I eat healthier, and all in all, I feel better than I did before I went out for that first jog.

By changing one thing, I changed my entire life for the better. By making one healthful little change, I raised my health consciousness to a new level. Once I did that, I began living my life in a completely different way.

This happens because a person's life is a totally integrated system. Everything is related to everything else. Your thoughts affect your health, your health affects your relationships, your relationships affect your point of view, your point of view affects your thoughts. That's why you can't change just one thing. It's the truth, and in this truth you'll find a powerful tool for raising your prosperity consciousness—a tool you can start using immediately.

DRESSING FOR SUCCESS

Okay, you realize that in order to achieve prosperity you must raise your prosperity consciousness. You've learned that by changing one thing in your life, you can eventually change everything. Now what do you do?

Earlier, when you fixed up your car—or apartment,

or whatever you chose—and got that prosperous feeling, you experienced an internal shift, an alteration in your prosperity consciousness. As a result of the change, you are now different, *inside*.

In the car exercise, you caused an *internal* change to occur by altering *external* conditions. This time you're going to do things the other way around: You're going to change your *external* circumstances to reflect the change that has occurred *within you*. Even though you may have experienced prosperity for only a few brief moments, you like the feeling and you want to re-create it. How?

I suggest that every day you do *some*thing—one small thing—that's symbolic of the new you. Something noticeable. Something that says on the outside what's going on inside Something that points in the direction you're now heading.

In his 1975 book, *Dress for Success*, John T. Molloy reported on some amazing discoveries he had made in his work as a "wardrobe engineer." He found that in business, not only is appearance important, but how a person dresses may actually make the difference between success and failure. People who dress like executives, Molloy said, are more likely to be considered for executive positions, while people who don't dress that way will probably not be promoted, no matter how capable they are.

You might think it's unfair that someone who's bright, competent and ambitious will be passed over for promotion just because he or she has a poor wardrobe. You could be right; maybe it *is* unfair. But according to Molloy, that's the way it is in the real world. You can complain about it, you can fight it or you can use this information to help boost your prosperity.

I know a woman who used this one idea as a spring-board for an entire career. Here's what happened.

In 1981, I started doing work for a new client, a medium-sized but rapidly growing consulting firm. Since I worked closely with these people, I spent a lot of time in their offices and learned a lot about their business. In this company, there were essentially two levels of employees: the professionals, most of whom were college graduates, male and over thirty-five, and the clerical staff, most of whom were high school or business school graduates, female and under thirty-five. The gap between these two levels was quite wide, and in the four or five years the company had been in business before I started working with it, no one had made the jump from clerical to professional.

Besides the contrasts mentioned above, the two groups differed in the way they dressed. The professionals, consisting of company executives and consultants, all came to work in suits. The clericals dressed in a variety of ways—from jeans and T-shirts in the word processing room to skirts and blouses among the executive secretaries.

Shortly after I began calling on the firm, a woman named Elizabeth was hired as a word processor. She was in her late twenties, bright, outgoing, with a wry sense of humor. I met her in the coffee room a few times, and we chatted, mostly about the firm and how busy everyone was.

Once I remarked about the sharp division between the two kinds of employees, and she agreed, but she pointed out that at that time a third kind of employee was beginning to emerge: the female professional. I didn't realize it then, but Elizabeth had made up her mind to join the ranks of the third group.

Women were filling the professional ranks because the firm was growing so fast that when a department expanded, the most capable clerical people were given supervisory and then managerial jobs. Also, some of the women who had been assisting the field consultants for a few years became so knowledgeable, they began handling consulting assignments alone. Elizabeth noticed that when these women moved into the professional level, they started wearing suits.

A few months of sitting at a word processor convinced Elizabeth she wanted more out of life. Since she was caring for her invalid mother, she couldn't afford the time or the tuition for college. She wasn't working for one of the consultants, so she couldn't move up by that route. And since all the executive secretarial jobs were filled, all she could do was apply for one, and wait.

But Elizabeth was ambitious—and impatient. She decided (without having read *Dress for Success*, by the way) that even if she wasn't actually an executive, she could at least look like one. So she saved her money, shopped very carefully and bought a conservative, professional-looking outfit consisting of a tailored coat, two skirts (one matching, one contrasting), a blouse and a couple of those ribbonlike ties professional women were wearing back then.

She started wearing her new clothes to work, even though in the word processing room, there was absolutely no need to. The other word processors ribbed her a bit; some even scoffed at her for wasting her money and effort. Of course, because her new outfits were so limited, she couldn't dress like an executive any more than a few days a week. Even so, the professional look made an impact. When she walked down the halls, executives who had previously paid no attention to her began to notice.

"Who was that?" they'd ask each other when she passed by. Some thought she was a newly hired manager; others figured she must be a client or a visitor from another firm.

The people she worked with in the word processing room began to regard her differently. "She won't be in here for long," they'd remark when Elizabeth came in looking especially sharp. In their eyes, her appearance was saying, "I'm here now, but I'm headed somewhere else." Yet in fact, nothing else had changed. Her name had not moved up on the promotion list. She still did the same work every day.

Then one day she caught a break. The executive vice-president had scheduled a big meeting in the conference room. An important client was coming to town, and several senior consultants were flying in from the field to confer about the client's problem. At such meetings, it was important to have a secretary on hand to take notes, make copies, order in lunch—all the little things no one notices unless they're not done.

About eight in the morning, the EVP's secretary called in at the last minute and said she was stuck at home with a dead battery. It was too late to call a temp service, and all the other secretaries were overloaded. The human resources manager, whose job it was to find a replacement, was wandering around the building, looking for someone—anyone—to fill in. Every minute that went by, she got more anxious. She burst into the coffee room and saw a group of women gathered about, filling their cups and getting ready to start their workday. One of the women caught her eye. It was Elizabeth, who happened to be wearing her conservative blue suit, crisp white blouse and paisley tie. With that outfit, she'd fit right in with the executives, the manager figured, and even though she wasn't actually a trained secretary, if she kept her ears open and followed instructions, she could get by.

"Liz, you're a lifesaver," the human resources manager said. "Can you assist at the EVP's meeting today? I'll get your boss to spread your work among the others."

Well, Elizabeth did a lot more than just get by. She performed so well, the EVP asked her to assist at a follow-up meeting the next day. That led to a temporary assignment backing up one of the consultants, which led to a permanent administrative assistant's job (the firm later eliminated the term "secretary") and finally some work as a "junior consultant" on small projects. As she moved through those jobs, she spent a lot of time with executives, clients and other consultants. She always wore a suit, and she asked the professionals a lot of questions. When someone sitting next to you, dressed in a serious suit, asks an intelligent question, it's hard not to answer. In this way, she learned. And the more she learned, the more valuable she became.

Today, Elizabeth is a senior consultant with a full-time assistant, a large office and enough frequent-flier miles to travel to the moon and back, first class, for free. She now has more invested in her wardrobe than many people pay for their cars, but she doesn't skimp when she goes shopping because she remembers how large a role her clothes played in her success.

SYMBOL OF THE NEW YOU

Elizabeth's story teaches us an important lesson, and it suggests a path you can take to your own prosperity. Notice Elizabeth didn't make a major change in her life. She didn't quit her job and go earn a college degree. She didn't buy a whole new wardrobe and drown herself in debt. All she did was raise her consciousness with regard to dress: She began dressing not for the job she *held*, but for the job she *wanted*. That one minor change, regularly applied over an extended period of time, ultimately had a major impact on her professional life.

While her appearance may seem like a superficial thing, it was actually a reflection of a more profound change that had taken place within her. When she made an internal decision to get promoted, her consciousness shifted. The change of clothes was an outgrowth of that shift.

I recommend that you do something similar. Make a small change in your appearance, a change that won't cost much and won't take much effort, but will have a significant meaning to you. Look at the shoes you wear to work. Are they clean, shined and repaired? If not, clean and shine them. Take one pair in and have new soles and heels put on. After a while, take another pair in and do the same. Eventually, have all your work shoes upgraded in this way.

Before you go to work every day, be sure your shoes are shined. That's all; nothing else. Do only that, but do it scrupulously every day. Make those shiny shoes a symbol of the new you, an outward sign of the prosperous attitude that's been germinating inside you since you first started reading this book.

A single change may or may not produce a noticeable result. That's all right; be patient. Remember, prosperity consciousness grows from within, so at first the only changes you need to be concerned about are those going on inside. As you become more careful about the appearance of your shoes, you'll become more careful about other things: your hair, your makeup, the rest of your clothing. The changes in you will become more noticeable. You'll be sending a message to the world that you're serious about your work, you're committed, you're on your way somewhere. When you walk by, people will start whispering things like, "Have you noticed? There's something different about Jack (or Jill) lately. He (she) seems more together, more on top of things."

You may never hear these whispers. You may not know your name is coming up more often when the managers talk about candidates for special assignments or promotions. But as you raise your prosperity consciousness, such things will start to happen. It's inevitable. If you change the image you project, people will change their opinion of you. It will be virtually impossible for them *not* to. If the change is an improvement, their opinion of you will improve as well.

When that happens, my friend, you're on the brink of producing permanent prosperity in your life. And to get yourself over that brink, there's one important rule you have to know.

You Have to Give Before You Get

"You must sow the seed, before you can reap the harvest."

—SCOTT REED

Let's go back again to the little weed lot where you grew beans. I want to draw another, somewhat obvious lesson from that example. It's so obvious, you might feel I'm being condescending by pointing it out. Obvious or not, so many people seem to have missed this idea, I'll risk dropping a reminder.

When you went out to the weed lot for beans, you didn't just demand the beans and get them. The earth doesn't work that way. You have to *give* something to the earth before you get something back. You have to give it seeds and water and time and attention. Then, and only then, will the earth give you beans.

I've been an employer long enough to know that people forget this lesson when it comes to their work. Rather than trying to find out what they can *give* to their employer, they focus on what they can expect to *get*.

In a job interview, the average applicant is a bundle of questions: "What's the salary? What are the benefits? How many paid holidays? Do you offer dental?" Salary reviews sound like this: "I haven't had a raise in nine months; I'm overdue." "I've been here four years; Jim's been here three years, so I should be making more than he is." "I could get more money than this working somewhere else."

Goodrich & Sherwood, a New York human resources management consulting firm, advises employees to develop a "value-added package" to present to either existing or prospective employers. This package, they say, has less to do with your work history than with your personal values, temperament, interests and skills both on and off the job. Once you've identified these, you can show how your skills, processes and point of view can make a real contribution. In a tight market, where many highly qualified people are competing for the same jobs, those who bring the most value to the table are the ones most likely to be hired, promoted or given a raise.

But you have to be willing to give the added value first. This might mean taking less money than you want initially, or agreeing to delay your raise until you can link it to improved productivity. It might even mean working for free until you prove your worth.

In my business, I buy a lot of printing, and one of the salesmen who calls on me has had a career that perfectly illustrates this principle. Scott was a job estimator at a large, ninety-year-old printing company. He liked his work, but it was getting repetitive, and he could see it wasn't leading anywhere. What he really wanted was to get into sales. He became a service representative so he could learn how to work with customers directly. After a year of this, he approached the sales manager and asked for a selling job. The manager clapped him on the shoulder and said, "Scott, I admire your ambition. But frankly, you're not a sales type; you're a production type. You're good at what you do. Relax, enjoy it and stay with it."

Scott realized the only way he would get a sales position was if he proved himself. So he took a succession of jobs with smaller printers, working on straight commission. Since he had no experience, no one was willing to give him more to start than some business cards and a pat on the back. For about eighteen months, he made cold calls, got rejected, fell on his face and learned everything the hard way. In one of his jobs, not only did he have to get the order, he also had to make the plates, run the press, deliver the finished product and collect the money.

After eighteen months, Scott had a track record, a clientele and, most important of all, the knowledge that he could do the job. He called the sales manager at his old company again, and described what he had accomplished and what he was now capable of doing. Two weeks later, he got an offer. It was straight commission, and it was contingent upon Scott bringing a certain number of clients with him. But it was the job he wanted.

Today, Scott makes a little over 300 percent more money than he would have if he'd taken the sales manager's advice and stayed in his old job. He's happily married to a nurse, whom he admits he wouldn't have had the confidence to ask out before his success in sales. He has his own sailboat, a Mercedes with a phone in it and the smile of a man who loves what he's doing. He's prosperous, by any definition.

A few years ago, when he first wanted to move into sales, it would have been easy for Scott to say, "I tried to better myself, but they wouldn't give me a chance." We've all known people who tell that kind of story. Maybe one of them is holding this book. But the past doesn't matter, because now you know it's not what "they" give you that determines whether you'll be prosperous or not; it's what *you* give. And you have to give before you can get. It's the law of nature—ask anyone who's ever grown beans.

WHERE DO YOU START CREATING VALUE?

No matter what your goals are, no matter where you want to end up, you have to start where you are. That's another law of nature. So take stock of your present situation, and start identifying opportunities to create value, right now.

Let's look at the simplest scenario. You work in a place where the normal hours are from 8:00 A.M. until 5:00 P.M., with an hour off for lunch. Suppose you, like everyone else, fudge a little on the work hours. You come in a few minutes late; to beat the rush at quitting time, you sometimes duck out a few minutes early. No big deal. No one reprimands you for it, so nothing is lost.

Now let's approach this with the laws of prosperity in mind. If you're being paid for eight hours but you work less than eight, you're not delivering full value. This is not a moral judgment, it's just the truth. To get started on the road to prosperity, make it a point to come in on time and leave on time. Every day. Give a full day's work for a full day's pay. Give your employers their money's worth. Just by doing this, you'll increase your value. In the process, it will bring you even. At the end of the week, you don't owe them the minutes you would have if you'd come in late or left early. Once they hand over your check, they don't owe you anything either. Nothing extraordinary here, just a straight, simple contract.

The next step is where the extraordinary stuff, the magic, happens. Start coming in early. Not much, five or ten minutes will do, fifteen is better. You don't have to change your work activities at all. Just come in early, and watch what happens.

Naturally, you won't want to waste those extra minutes, so you might use them to straighten your work area, make some coffee, catch up on your required reading, get ready for the day. When eight o'clock comes, you'll "hit the ground running," and be more productive from the very first minute. You may find the extra fifteen minutes saves you an hour of scrambling to get started after everyone else has arrived.

After you've been coming in early for a while, people will begin to notice. Predictably, some of your coworkers will fault you for it, accusing you of trying to make them look bad, or of causing your employers to expect everyone to do the same. If this happens, you have a choice: Are you going to listen to these people, and revert to their way of working, or will you continue on your new path? The answer is another question: Will you be satisfied with their level of prosperity? Is your prosperity consciousness on a par with theirs? If not, this may be where you break out of the ranks of those who do as little as possible just to get by.

Soon your employers will start noticing your new work hours. At first, they might be suspicious. They might even ask you why you're doing this. When you answer, it's important to make it clear that you're just *giving* more, not expecting more in return.

You can say, "I find I can just get a lot more done when I have a head start." Or, "There's so much to learn; the extra time helps me keep up with new information."

Don't say you're bucking for a raise, because in truth, that's not what you're doing. You're trying to learn what you need to know to operate at a higher level—a level where people make more money. Besides, your employers already know everyone wants a raise, but they've seen that no one's willing to do anything extra to get it. The fact that you're doing more, and not asking for more in return, sets you apart from all the rest.

As time goes on, a "debt" will build up. Your employers will owe you for all those extra unpaid minutes you put in. Don't ever ask to be compensated for them; no one told you to put in the time. Don't ever complain about how you work extra without extra pay; that would just put you back in the ranks of the whiners. Just let the debt accumulate. Sooner or later, you'll collect on it. When the time comes for raises and promotions, who do you think will get first consideration? When someone's putting together a team to handle an exciting new project, who will be chosen?

If the decision were up to you, who would you promote, the person who comes in a few minutes late every day, or the one who comes in a few minutes early? Who would you want on your team—the one who gets a head start, or the one who's always a step behind?

What if your current employers don't notice or don't reward this kind of behavior? Relax, the debt you're running up is universal—if it's not paid by them, it will be paid by someone else. Remember my friend Hans, the mortgage banker? His employer was too shortsighted to reward him properly. But not everyone's that shortsighted.

To appreciate what I'm saying here, you have to accept the principle of circulation. This principle holds that when you put out, you get back. In biblical terms, "As ye sow, so shall ye reap." In more modern terms, "What goes around, comes around." Those who deny the validity of this principle are those who refuse to take a wide enough view. When you give, you get back—although you don't necessarily get it back right away, and then not necessarily from those you gave to.

If you give, just do it—not with strings attached, but with the conviction that you'll one day, in some way, get back that much or more. Do it, and you'll have a life of ever-growing, ever-expanding prosperity. I can't prove this to you, but I can give you many examples of people who have used this principle successfully. Personally, I use it all the time, and the rewards are absolutely amazing. But to experience the truth of it, you'll have to try it yourself.

MORE WAYS TO CREATE VALUE

So far in your drive to create value, all you've done is show up a little earlier, and maybe work a little more. To really create prosperity, start improving the *quality* of your work. How? You ought to know; after all, it's your job. If you don't know, use the "modeling" technique I described in Chapter 7. Identify the people in your organization or your job classification who are known for the quality of their work. Approach them; ask them how they do it. Nearly everyone who's good at his or her work loves to talk about it. If you can't approach these people in person, call them on the phone, write to them, read the articles they write, go hear them speak. Soon their information and advice will start to pay off as your skills and abilities increase.

Again, as all this is happening, don't ask for anything in return. Just give; don't try to get. Produce better results, higher output, more quality for the same pay. And watch what happens. If your employers are unenlightened, they'll think you a fool and try to keep getting more from you without paying for it. If that's the case, you'll soon find out, and you can start looking for employers who are willing to give value for value received. But don't expect your employers to take unfair advantage of you. It's far more likely that they'll be delighted with your new level of productivity and more than happy to reward you for it.

If you're in business for yourself and you want to increase your prosperity, add a new feature or an extra benefit to your product or service, but don't add to the cost. Smart customers will soon notice that your business is providing greater value, and they'll start coming to you. There's nothing revolutionary about this idea. It's one of the most basic techniques of commerce, yet so many businesses have forgotten it, we're actually amazed when we see it in action.

Quite a few years ago, as pizza delivery companies were sprouting up everywhere, one man got a bright idea for adding value: When a customer called to order a pizza, he would deliver *two* for the same price. His competitors said he was crazy. They said he'd go broke. Well, he wasn't crazy and today Little Caesar's is far from broke.

Shaken out of its complacency, the American auto industry is relearning the lesson of this chapter. According to *The Wall Street Journal* of June 4, 1992, the Big Three have turned the tables and are starting to take market share away from the Japanese (2 percent in a single year). How? By increasing quality and producing cars with fewer defects. By appealing to market niches with four-wheel drive vehicles, minivans and light trucks. By pricing aggressively while Japanese automakers contend with high domestic wages and a strong yen. The combination of significantly increased value and no significant increase in price is making the American auto industry prosperous again.

If value can be created by large corporations, it can certainly be done by individuals—and much more easily. In 1992, I took an extremely worthwhile course whose purpose was to help people take complete control of the financial aspect of their lives. It was called The Finance Course, and it was created by a man named Roger Lane. At the beginning of the course, we all wrote down what we wanted to accomplish financially. Roger told me later that on average, people aim to increase their income or sales between 50 and 100 percent by the end of the six-week course.

One of the most important lessons in the course involved listing all the products and/or services each of us provided, and then trying to come up with ways to increase the value of those products and services. To do this, most of us simply brainstormed by ourselves, or asked for suggestions from members of the group. We didn't hire high-priced consultants or do extensive research. We just gave the issue some attention. The result was amazing. Everyone came away bubbling with ideas for improving quality, increasing efficiency, boosting productivity, making customers happy—more ideas than we could possibly use.

According to Roger's records, as of 1993, over seven thousand people had completed The Finance Course, and over 95 percent of them had achieved their goals. Is there a magic secret? I asked Roger, and his reply was simple. "You have to *serve* people," he said. "You've got to make their lives easier, or better, or more worth living. This is true whether you're offering a product or a service. The product or service must *serve* people in the sense that it benefits them, enhances them in some way. Then they'll want to reward you for it by giving you money."

To translate this message into the terms we're using in this book, you must *create value* for people. You must *deliver value* so they benefit from it. And you must *accept value* in return.

In this way, you put the Secret to work. You choose your road to prosperity and you pave it with value. From here on, nothing can stop you.

CHAPTER 10

What If Your Prosperity Goes Away?

"I've never been poor, only broke. Being poor is a frame of mind. Being broke is only a temporary situation."

—MIKE TODD

My purpose in writing this book is to help people become prosperous and stay prosperous for the rest of their lives. I know this can be done. I've been personally familiar with many people who've accomplished it, some of whom I've mentioned in these pages. But I also know prosperity can be lost. The clogged dockets of bankruptcy courts in every state are all the evidence we need that prosperity isn't necessarily permanent.

Prosperity can be destroyed in three ways:
1. By delivering value, and not receiving value in return.
2. By accepting value, and not delivering value in return.
3. By consuming more than you produce.

1. By delivering value, and not receiving value in return.

Whenever you deliver value to someone, you use up resources: time, energy, money, materials. None of them are infinite. Eventually, they run out. If you consume limited resources to produce value, and don't receive enough in return to replenish what you've used, sooner or later you'll lose the capacity to produce.

Many a misguided wealthy person has made the mistake of giving full value but not insisting on getting full value in return, only to see a lifetime's accumulation of wealth slowly disappear. There's nothing wrong with charitable giving. I'm a big believer in it, and give as much as I can. Nearly all the wealthy people I know give generously. It's a marvelous way to use and benefit from the law of circulation. But you must understand that the world is not one gigantic charity. *Some*body has to pay you for what you create. If they don't, in time you won't have anything left to give to those who need and can't pay. So always monitor what's coming in and how much you're keeping in net pay or profit. This is what keeps you prosperous. It keeps you financially healthy and able to create value another day.

2. By accepting value, and not delivering value in return.

You see this in businesses that become successful by giving customers their money's worth, but then let quality and service slip, causing value to drop while prices stay up. Individuals are just as guilty of this. I've known salespeople who hustle for years to build up a territory or account list, then grow complacent and assume their customers will stay loyal forever. They don't keep in touch. They show up late for appointments. They don't put in the extra effort that won the customer in the first place. And before long, the customer is gone.

No matter what occupation you're in, you're vulnerable to this phenomenon. When you're on a salary, and protected by a union or a civil service board, it's easy to think all you have to do is show up and put in your time. But in the same way you earn universal credits by doing more than you're paid for, you also build up a debt to the universe by doing less. Sooner or later, that debt has to be repaid, and only you can repay it. Maybe not to that employer, and maybe not in money, but in one way or another. There are many people drawing paychecks who mistakenly think they're defying this principle. Not only are they cheating themselves out of the rewarding experience of doing a job well, they're cheating themselves out of prosperity.

To stay prosperous, you must constantly monitor your output, making sure that whoever is paying you is getting value. If not, you have to create new value, or eventually accept pay that more closely reflects your contribution.

3. By consuming more than you produce.

If you grow beans, harvest and eat them all, then rip out the plants and eat them too, you'll soon be without the means to grow another bean. If, on the other hand, you sell some of the beans so that you can afford to water and fertilize, and if you save some of the beans to use as seeds, you keep the ability to produce beans indefinitely.

One of the most basic laws of economics is that you can't spend more than you take in. No matter how successful you are, no matter how much value you create and how much value you receive in return, violate that law and you're bound to go broke. If you make a dollar and spend ninety cents, you can be prosperous forever; if you make a dollar and spend $1.10, your prosperity days are numbered.

There you have the three destroyers of prosperity. Every other way of becoming unprosperous, whether by increments or catastrophe, is a variation of one of these. And no one is immune to them. Whatever can be created can be destroyed, whatever can be won can be lost. So what do you do if your prosperity goes away? Jump out of a building, as so many did when the market crashed in 1929? Take to the streets and beg for spare change, as so many do today? No, you rediscover what got you started in the first place: your prosperity consciousness.

REDISCOVERING YOUR PROSPERITY CONSCIOUSNESS

Let's go back to a concept we explored extensively in the beginning of this book—the idea that money and prosperity are not the same thing. We looked at a number of people who were prosperous, but had little or no money. We found that it was something inside them—their prosperity consciousness—that made them prosperous. We also learned that if you develop your prosperity consciousness, actual prosperity is sure to follow.

I believe that when people suffer major financial setbacks, it's because they've lost touch with their prosperity consciousness. Why and how they happen to suffer the loss will vary greatly from one individual to another. Some people sabotage their own success—for deep-seated reasons they can't understand. Some are just plain careless and let the money slip away. Some are unfortunate enough to lose everything in an accident, fire or hurricane.

Regardless of why or how the loss occurred, we should not look upon it as final. Instead, we can characterize it as a "temporary misplacement of prosperity consciousness." When we think of a setback in that way, it's not nearly as devastating. As long as you have your prosperity consciousness, you can become prosperous again. The amount of money you actually possess is irrelevant.

The quote at the beginning of this chapter is attributed to Mike Todd, a successful innovator in the movie industry during the middle of the twentieth century. When he said, "I've never been poor, only broke," he meant that while he often lost his money, he never lost his prosperity consciousness, and thus was always able to make his money back. Even if you do misplace your prosperity consciousness, you can always rediscover it, and when you do, based on what you now know, you can immediately start back on the road to permanent prosperity.

A client of mine had a life-shattering experience that illustrates this point dramatically. As a young woman, Bobbi DePorter made a great deal of money in the real estate business. When she started selling real estate, her employer gave her a target of $30,000 income in her first year. She made $30,000 the first *day*. As a broker, she once cleared $850,000 from a single condominium conversion. Within five years, she had a net worth of over $2 million, and she was barely thirty years old.

Then she and her partner met a college professor who had a system for playing the stock options market. He convinced them of the validity of this system, and they tried it. The system worked so well, and they made so much money, they were able to buy a seat on the options exchange. They shared the system with other investors, and made the mistake of guaranteeing these investors that they would not lose money.

Well, no system is foolproof, as they found out. The market turned, and in a shockingly short time they were wiped out. Bobbi and her partner not only lost their entire investment, but they also had to make good the losses of the other investors. When all the lawsuits were settled, Bobbi had all of her real estate and most of her personal belongings taken from her. Her children had to go live with her ex-husband. She even had to part with her beloved Saint Bernard. The only thing left was her car, which the lawyers had somehow overlooked. For a time, that car and a few things she carried in it were all she had in the world. She was literally homeless, relying on friends to take her in for a few days at a time.

Eventually, Bobbi landed at a friend's house in Los Angeles, where she was able to spend three months thinking and healing. After that quiet time, she began to get in touch with people again, and some former associates asked her if she wanted to help them start a business school. That and another venture blossomed for a while, then eventually folded; but they helped bring her back into the world, ready to start over. So she borrowed against the only thing of value she owned, her car, and opened an innovative summer school for teenagers, called SuperCamp. That was in 1982, and today her school is an international success. Every year, SuperCamp helps thousands of kids all over the world rediscover the joy of learning. And Bobbi, having created enormous value for people, is as prosperous as ever.

I asked Bobbi how this devastating loss made her feel. "At first, I felt guilty, because I'd lost so much money for people, and I'd let them down. I felt everyone hated me, and in fact, some of them did. Even good friends were afraid to be near me. It was as if my problem was contagious, and they'd lose money just by being with me. For a while the pain was paralyzing. I couldn't work, I couldn't even move."

Today, over a dozen years later, she looks upon the loss as one of the most valuable experiences in her life. "I feel stronger now, more my own person. I fear loss a lot less. I know you can lose and come out the other side. Before I went through it, the whole thing seemed horrendous. But afterwards, I realized that, if you can somehow push away the anxiety, your life is not much different going through a big loss than it is when you're going through a big gain.

"I found that, even without money, you can live *life*—you can find food and a place to stay, you can get by. All the really essential things are much the same as always."

The marvelous lesson we can learn from Bobbi's experience is that no matter how completely our prosperity consciousness seems to desert us, it doesn't go away. Once you've developed the quality in yourself that prosperity is made of, it's yours permanently. You may lose touch with it; you may forget you have it; you may even look poverty-stricken for years at a time. In the words of Mike Todd, you may be broke—but you'll never be poor.

What, then, do you do when your prosperity goes away? Create it all over again. Who knows, the next time may wind up being more fun.

What If You Hate Your Prosperity?

> *"Banks and riches are chains of gold, but still chains."*
>
> —EDMUND RUFFIN

In the hit movie *Trading Places*, Eddie Murphy and Dan Aykroyd play a couple of hotshots who make a killing in the commodities market, then dash off to a tropical island to enjoy their wealth. The film's final scene shows them lounging on the beach, accompanied by shapely young women, trying to decide whether to have steak or lobster for lunch. (They opt for both.)

This is the classic American notion of what "happily ever after" is supposed to look like: Make a fortune, head for paradise, live on the beach.

Can you imagine a more boring, brain-numbing existence than lounging aimlessly on some isolated strip of sand for months at a time? If the ultraviolet rays don't kill you, the cholesterol wallop from those steak-and-lobster combos certainly will.

Making money is not an end in itself. Having money is not necessarily enjoyable, and being wealthy can be a miserable experience. If money made people happy, every rich person would be ecstatic, and we know that's not so.

The truth is, anything that puts distance between you and what you really want has the potential to make you unhappy. If it's important to you to spend time with your family, and your new promotion keeps you away from home, how much good has the promotion actually done? If you enjoy bowling with the guys from the plant and your newly achieved affluence takes you out of their league, did you lose more than you gained?

In the single-minded pursuit of prosperity, it's easy to get fooled into thinking that making money is what it's all about. After all, the way we keep score is by counting the money. "He who dies with the most toys, wins"—right?

Maybe not. When you've achieved a level of financial success, but you're not happy with it, you know you've gone astray somewhere. This can be a devastating revelation. You think, "I worked so hard for this money, so many people want it. Why doesn't it make me feel better?" My teacher, Roger Lane, has the answer.

"Even though everyone's scrambling after money," he says, "that's not what they really want. Money itself is nothing—pieces of paper, numbers on a statement. What people want is *experiences*. They're scrambling for money because they believe money can help them get the experiences they're looking for."

Suppose you ardently love to skim over the open water with the wind in your hair and salt spray on your face. Money can buy you a boat, and the boat can give you the experience. However, if you make a lot of money, but are so busy you never get a chance to leave the city, what good will it do you to buy a boat? The money, and the boat itself, will become sources of frustration for you. Before long, you may be wondering why you're working so hard. It might be better to work less and use the extra free time to hitch rides on other people's boats.

BUILDING YOUR PROSPERITY OUT OF EXPERIENCES

Roger Lane's insight provides a valuable tool for building the kind of prosperity you want. Rather than building your prosperity out of money, possessions or power, you can build it out of the experiences that fill up your life.

To my mind, the only experiences that contribute to my prosperity are those that leave me better off—healthier, happier, more fulfilled. I measure my prosperity by the number and quality of these experiences. Some of them require money; some don't. Earlier today, I stopped writing this chapter and went to a baseball game—a real thriller, with my team winning dramatically in the bottom of the tenth inning. To be out there in the sun, enjoying baseball with a good friend, is an experience I value highly. But the ticket cost money, as did the parking and refreshments. Plus, I didn't earn any money the whole afternoon. I consider myself prosperous to be able to afford such an experience. By my definition, if I couldn't afford it, my prosperity would be diminished.

This evening, when Wanda and I have both finished working, we'll go for one of our three-mile walks. She'll tell me about her day, I'll recount every pitch of that climactic tenth inning, we'll make plans for dinner, and in the process we'll get some healthful exercise. That walk is another experience I cherish, yet it won't cost a dime. If instead of walking I worked tonight, I'd make money, but it couldn't begin to compensate for the lost experience. At the end of the evening, I'd be *wealthier, but less prosperous*.

It can be worthwhile to ask yourself, "Have I been trying to build my prosperity out of money? Have I been striving to make money in the belief that it's *the* way to become prosperous?" If you answer yes, I'm going to suggest you look at things differently from now on. Look at something in your life that makes you money, or costs you money. If it doesn't help to make you any happier, if it doesn't give you the *experience* you want, then get rid of it, no matter how wonderful you thought it would be.

Let's say you work hard and buy a fabulous new car, the one you've dreamed about since you were a teenager. But your workplace is in a high crime area, so every time you go to work, you have anxiety about the car being broken into or stolen. This anxiety diminishes, maybe even destroys the experience you were seeking when you bought the car. Possible solutions: Rent a secure parking space; take public transportation; drive a cheap used car to work and keep the new car safe at home. If none of these do the trick, then just sell the car and find some other way to create the experience it was supposed to give you.

The *experience* is what was going to make you feel prosperous in the first place. By taking this action, you're refusing to allow a material possession to take your prosperity away.

What I'm suggesting is not easy. It's hard to give up something you worked so hard for. If you've become accustomed to certain luxuries that putting in long hours has given you, it might seem hard to make do without them. But if those luxuries are keeping you from having the experiences you *really* want, you're better off doing the hard thing and getting them out of your life.

When you do that—when you build your prosperity around experiences rather than money—you're putting the emphasis in the right place, on the end or the goal, rather than the means. You're building your prosperity out of the right stuff. A prosperity you'll find hard to hate. A prosperity you'll want to keep in your life, permanently.

Believe In the System—It Always Works

> *"Plant a kernel of wheat and you reap a pint; plant a pint, and you reap a bushel. Always the law works to give you back more than you give."*
> —ANTHONY NORVELL

The planting of a seed is an act of faith. When a farmer entrusts a seed to the ground, he's showing his belief in the system. He believes he's going to get back something of greater value than the seed. When he adds water and nutrients to the soil, he's demonstrating his belief that by giving more, he'll get back more. If he didn't believe in the system, he'd hold on to the seed and try to get nutritional value from eating it.

Why does a farmer take this enormous risk? Why does he go through all the trouble to prepare the soil, plant the seed, water it, feed it—and then just let nature take over? What gives him so much confidence?

The farmer believes in the system because it always works. It always has worked, and it always will. Of course, floods, droughts and pests destroy crops. But these are contingencies he can deal with. Unpredictable elements are acceptable, as long as the system itself is predictable. And the system is completely predictable: seeds + soil + water + sun + nutrients = crops. Knowing that, the next time planting season comes around (as it *always* does), he plants. Once he plants, he walks away. He doesn't dig up the seeds to see if they know how to sprout. His confidence is complete, because the system is complete.

This same kind of system exists in business, or in any other endeavor that is a potential source of prosperity for you. At the heart of the system is the Secret: *To become prosperous, you must create value for people and accept value in return.* It always works. If you create value for people and accept value in return, you *will* become prosperous, no doubt about it. You can believe in it as completely as the farmer believes in his seeds.

In fact, to become prosperous, you *must* believe in it. Because if you don't, you'll never even start. And you must *keep* believing in it, or else you'll quit. Sure, things will go wrong. You'll have your share of floods, droughts and pests—in your field, perhaps they'll be layoffs, firings and bankruptcies. But those things don't invalidate the system. They don't mean the system doesn't work. On the contrary, they show how strong the system is, to work despite all that.

The farmer also knows he can't plant one crop and expect to live off it forever. He knows that to keep producing, he must keep planting, year after year. Even if he plants a perennial crop, he knows he must care for it constantly, and that when he stops caring for it, the abundance it produces will soon stop too.

Similarly, the Secret to Permanent Prosperity says you have to keep creating value and accepting value—for as long as you want your prosperity to last. As I write this, George Burns, the patriarch of entertainers, is over ninety-eight years old. Not only is he still working, he has a contract to appear in London on his one hundredth birthday. When he was asked how he was so sure he'd live to be a hundred, Burns reportedly replied, "I have to; I can't miss a booking."

Some years ago, Burns was asked when he was going to retire. "Never," he snapped. "Retirement is death." George Burns knows that the secret to his own prosperity is his work. Does he need the money? Of course not; he has more money than he could possibly spend. He works because it keeps him active, sharp, interested, happy. He works because through his work he creates value for people, and they give value back. He works because he believes in the system, and it has never failed him. For almost a century, with a cigar, an off-key song and a wisecrack, George Burns has lived the Secret to Permanent Prosperity.

You must believe in the system, even if it appears to have failed. When Bobbi DePorter borrowed against her only valuable possession to start a new business—after having lost millions less than two years before—she was demonstrating her belief in the system. She knew that if she created value for children and their parents, she would get value in return, and she would once again become prosperous. The system worked, and no one was *less* surprised than she.

When you believe in the system, you automatically take much of the anxiety out of your endeavors.

Of course, there will always be something to worry about. Farmers still worry about the weather, but they don't worry about their seeds doing the job. The system takes care of that. When business gets bad, you may still worry about cash flow. But you know that if you increase the value of your product or service, the market will respond and your cash flow will improve. The system takes care of that.

When you believe in the system, you know that if you continue to create more and more value, you'll be rewarded with more and more. It won't necessarily be in the form you expected, or at the time you expected, but it will come. It's inevitable. That's the system.

When you believe in the system, you work not for money, but for the experiences money can provide, and you find ways to get the experiences money can't buy. When you believe in the system, you use the Secret, building your prosperity from within yourself, reinforcing it, making it permanent. When you use the Secret, life becomes not a mindless pursuit of possessions, but a joyous adventure. And if you can make it that, what more could you possibly want?